The Cup and the Covenant

DR. VERN C. LEWIS

DEDICATION

This book is dedicated to the Ray and Barbara Brown Family,
life-long friends and supporters from Bible Study Fellowship days.
—VL

TABLE OF CONTENTS

PROLOGUE

The word *prologue* refers to an author's attempt to capture the interest of a reader or patron to the meaning and message that is forth coming in a book, poem, or a play. That certainly is true of this study of what has become known as *The Cup and the Covenant*. Voltaire once said, "To teach is to twice learn." As a former teacher, I have found that to be true when research is involved. Another wisdom that attracted my attention came from an old Talmudic saying: *Where there is no knowledge, there is no understanding.* The opposite is also true. *Where there is no understanding, there is no knowledge. There may be more to you than you are aware.*

When I read the toast that Jesus gave at the Last Supper I realized Christians know very little about the history and transfer of the New Covenant, intended for Israel, to the Church Jesus formed (see Matthew 16:18). Another mystery is the difference between the word *Church* as an organization, and the Church Jesus created as a body or family of God. What was different about the church Jesus said He was going to build in Matthew 16:18? It was rewarding to read the reaction of the Apostle Paul in gaining a personal understanding of those mysteries revealed to him after his conversion; *He and his co-workers were made competent ministers of the New Covenant.*

Both knowledge and understanding can be attained in these pages so full of scriptural proofs. *It is possible to be born again as a believer and still not know all the riches given to you in Christ. Learn what was revealed to Paul about the "mysteries" revealed to him!*

CHAPTER ONE

This Cup Is

The scene had been set by Jesus like a great director. He had arranged for an upper room with all the preparations available to spend this Passover meal with His disciples. That particular meal had a custom of using four cups to recall God's grace in the life-history of the Jews. When He got to the third cup, Jesus gave a toast that changed our lives. He lifted the cup and said, "This cup is the new covenant in my blood which is poured out for you." (Luke 22:20).

It was a perfect setting for Jesus to introduce a new cup metaphor that would have an effect on all our lives. Only Jesus knew that His Cup and the atonement He was about to make would introduce a new creation. It would no longer be a private possession just for the Jews. It would include the whole universe.

In any drama about to begin, a list of those involved should be made known, along with some background. With Jesus, there were twelve of His disciples at that feast. One of the twelve was called Judas Iscariot who was to be the one to betray Him later in the evening. He must have been reclining to the left of Jesus because the Apostle John was on His right. Only John would record that arrangement at a time just before the Passover meal started. Jesus told him that the one to whom He gave a piece of bread, dipped in one of the bowls, would be the betrayer. He saw Jesus give the dipped-bread to Judas Iscariot and heard the Lord tell him to go, do what he had planned (see John 13:23-27).

Judas left the group to go and tell the chief priests and others how they could quietly arrest Jesus later that night on the Mount of Olives. It would be easier than risking the possibility of upsetting people that had gathered in Jerusalem for the observance of Passover. It is obvious that He was not present when the toast was given. The rest of the group thought Jesus had asked Judas, their treasurer, to give something to the poor, for that was customary during the Passover. The eleven that remained were named:

Simon (who is called Peter) and his brother Andrew; James son of Zebedee, and his brother John; Philip and Bartholomew; Thomas and Matthew the tax collector; James son of Alphaeus, and Thaddaeus; and Simon the Zealot... (Matthew 10:2-4 NIV)

A brief outline of the procedure for a Passover meal helps to understand some of the cup metaphors used during the proceedings. This practice had been observed yearly on the tenth day of Abib, the first month of the Jewish calendar, ever since the night of the Exodus from Egypt. After a feast of unleavened bread, a year-old lamb without defect was to be slaughtered and its blood swabbed on the door lintels and posts as a sign for the death angel to pass over that house on that night. The meat of the lamb was to be eaten inside the house without any bones being broken. The sequential order for the Passover Meal was set by Moses:

"You shall also observe the Feast of Unleavened Bread, for on this very day I brought your hosts out of the land of Egypt; therefore you shall observe this day through-out your generations as a permanent ordinance. In the first month, on the fourteenth day of the month at eve-ning, you shall eat unleavened bread, until the twenty-first day of the month at evening. Seven days there shall be no leaven found in your houses; for whoever eats what is leavened, that person shall be cut off from the congregation of Israel, whether he is an alien or a native of the land. You shall not eat anything leavened; in all your dwellings you shall eat unleavened bread." Then Moses called for all the elders of Israel and said to them, "Go and take for yourselves lambs according to your families, and slay the Passover lamb. You shall take a bunch of hyssop and dip it in the blood which is in the basin, and apply some of the blood that is in the basin to the lintel and the two doorposts; and none of you shall go outside the door of his house until morning. For the LORD will pass through to smite the Egyptians; and when He sees the blood on the lintel and on the two doorposts, the LORD will pass over the door and will not allow the destroyer to come in to your houses to smite you. And you shall observe this event as an ordinance for you and your children forever. When you enter the land which the LORD will give you, as He has promised, you shall observe this rite. And when your children say to you, 'What does this rite mean to you?' you shall say, 'It is a Passover sacrifice to the LORD who passed over the houses of the sons of Israel in Egypt when He smote the Egyptians, but spared our homes.'" And the people bowed low and worshiped. Then the sons of Israel went and did so; just as the LORD had commanded Moses and Aaron, so they did. (Exodus 12:17-28 NASB)

To their credit, committed Jews still honor this day, second only to Yom Kippor (The Day of Atonement). It was vital to their memory of the flight from Egypt and of the old covenant they had agreed to keep. Rabbis and elders created a pattern to meet the decrees of Moses. A series of readings are selected by a leader from the book of Exodus concerning the Passover. After each reading, one of the following questions is asked:

a. *What does this meal mean?*

b. *Why is this night different?*

c. *Why on this night do we only eat unleavened bread?*

d. *Why are we eating bitter herbs?*

After each question the leader provides some explanation of the reading, after which a cup of wine is shared:

a. The first cup is offered as a benediction, or *kadesh*.

b. The second cup is offered at the end of the answer to the second question, called *The Haggadah*.

c. The third cup is offered after a prayer is recited for the meal, followed by an offering of the third cup. It was called *The Cup of Redemption*.

d. A fourth cup was called *The Cup of Elijah*, that was laid aside for the coming of the prophet.

The End of the Last Supper

Jesus was raising the third cup when He made His statement (see Luke 22:20). If this were a sermon, I would call it *The Cup Metaphors*. Each phrase in the statement Jesus made will be used as the title of the first four chapters. Jesus was sent to be more than the Lamb that takes away the sins of all who believe in Him. He was also given the role of being the other Lamb that provided the blood to mediate the covenant. The first phrase, *This Cup is,* was a preview of the entire means whereby God was going to create new natures that would be eternally righteous and totally forgiven for all who are willing to accept His offer of grace. A new covenant from God would emerge from that cup of suffering.

What a moment it was in history! It is doubtful those who were there that evening fully understood what He meant. We have no idea of the stress Jesus was experiencing in knowing how He was going to die. He gave us a clue in His use of the word *Cup* as a metaphor. When He said, "This Cup is" He was referring to the suffering that would be necessary to introduce and offer God's new covenant to the world.

He was using a metaphor to stand for all that He was about to suffer the next day. On the way to the Last Supper, He had used the word *cup* with James and John, the sons of Zebedee, who had the nerve to ask Jesus to seat them on each side of Him in heaven. He must have thought them audacious to make such a request, for He answered, "You don't know what you are asking!" He gave them an illustration placed in a question: "Can you drink the cup I drink or be baptized with the baptism I am baptized with?" "We can," they answered. Knowing their future martyrdoms, He agreed: "You will drink the cup I drink and be baptized with the baptism I am baptized with." He was referring to the baptism of the Holy Spirit raising Him from the grave. He knew they would experience that same baptism one day.

When Jesus raised the cup, it represented His *physical suffering*. That was not all Jesus had in His cup. He would have *mental suffering* from the thought of having the sins of the world placed upon Him. John the Baptist knew about it. In John 1:29, he told his disciples that: "Jesus was the Lamb of God who would take away the sins of the world." (He was identifying Jesus as the scapegoat). Jesus also may have been thinking about the words of the prophet Isaiah:

But he was pierced for our transgressions, he was crushed for our iniquities; the punishment that brought us peace was on him, and by his wounds we are healed. We all, like sheep, have gone astray, each of us has turned to our own way; and the LORD has laid on him the iniquity of us all. (Isaiah 53:5-6 NIV)

The mental suffering was verified later as He prayed on the Mount of Olives. Both Matthew and John who were there described what took place. Matthew said that Jesus took Peter and the sons of Zebedee aside with Him saying: "My soul is overwhelmed with sorrow to the point of death." Jesus fell to His knees and prayed: "Father, if you are willing, take this cup from Me; yet not my will, but yours be done." He was anticipating all that was about to happen. Luke was told that an angel appeared and strengthened Him as He began to pray more earnestly. The Lord's sweat looked like drops of blood falling to the ground. He suffered mentally beyond our comprehension. He knew His time had come to finish what the Father had sent Him to accomplish.

When He finished praying, He returned to the others just as Judas with some soldiers and officials arrived to arrest Him. Peter, without thinking, drew his sword to defend Him. In John 18:11, Jesus told him to put his sword away saying: "Shall I not drink the cup the Father has given Me?" The soldiers bound Jesus and took Him to a former High Priest who began an illegal interrogation late that night. After He had suffered mentally in the garden, the physical suffering began as the High Priest sought to trap him into a charge of blasphemy. One of the officials struck him in the face (see John 18:22). Remember that He was helplessly bound all this time! Most of us who saw Mel Gibson's movie, *The Passion of The Christ*, had difficulty looking at the face and body of Jesus after the interrogations.

At the break of dawn they took Him as a criminal to the palace of the Roman governor, Pilate. He asked for evidence of any crime Jesus had committed. They had no answer. He suggested they judge Him according to their own law. The Jews put the burden back on Pilate by saying they had no right under Roman law to execute anyone. John wrote that this happened so that scriptural predictions of how Messiah would die would be fulfilled (18:32). Jesus was to be crucified.

When Pilate asked Jesus, "Are you then king of the Jews?," He answered that His kingdom was not of this world. Pilate saw the possibility of a crime when he said, "You are a king then!" It was a Roman law that no one could claim to be king other than Caesar. The crime was so minor in Pilate's eyes, he offered to release Him to the Jews, but they refused.

To protect himself from any criticism, Pilate had Jesus flogged unmercifully. He allowed the soldiers to put a crown of thorns on His head and clothed Him in a purple robe. He offered to release Jesus once again as a Passover pardon, but the Jews refused again, crying out, "Crucify! Crucify!" They added that Jesus had even claimed to be the Son of God. When the chief priests also said, "We have no king but Caesar," Pilate finally allowed Jesus to be judged as a criminal to be crucified.

The criminal cup and the cup of suffering applied to Him. They were both fulfilled by Jesus on the cross. All four gospels must be read to get the full account. The greatest suffering took place between the sixth hour (noon) and the ninth hour (3 pm). Both Matthew and Mark reported that darkness came over the area during those three hours.

At the ninth hour Jesus was heard to say, "My God, My God, why have you forsaken Me?" In John 19:30, His last words were: "It is finished!" With that He bowed His head and gave up His spirit. At that point the curtain in front of the Holy of Holies was torn from top to bottom. The people felt the earth shake to the point graves were opened and rocks were split.

Since the next day was a special Passover Sabbath, the bodies were removed leaving only the blood spattered crosses. They asked Pilate to make sure the men crucified with Jesus were dead so the bodies could be removed. Soldiers broke the legs of the robbers to make sure they were dead. When they came to Jesus, He appeared to be dead already, so they did not break his legs. Instead a soldier came forward with a spear to prove the Lord was dead. He knew that if He were dead, water and blood would flow out of His abdomen once the heart had stopped pumping and circulating the blood.

John reported the significance of what happened:

But when they came to Jesus and found that he was already dead, they did not break his legs. Instead, one of the soldiers pierced Jesus' side with a spear, bringing a sudden flow of blood and water. The man who saw it has given testimony, and his testimony is true. He knows that he tells the truth, and he testifies so that you also may believe. These things happened so that the scripture would be fulfilled: "Not one of his bones will be broken," and, as another scripture says, "They will look on the one they have pierced." (John 19:33-37 NIV; cf. Exodus 12:46; Numbers 9:12; Psalm 34:20)

The water and the blood that gushed out was a fulfillment of the phrase *poured out for you.* A life was required for redemption from sin under the Law.

For the life of a creature is in the blood, and I have given it to you to make atonement for yourselves on the altar; it is the blood that makes atonement for one's life. (Leviticus 17:11 NIV)

It was the value of the Lord's life that enabled a new truth to be stated: "He died for the sins of the whole world."

For God so loved the world, that he gave his only begotten Son, that whosoever believeth in him should not
perish, but have everlasting life. (John 3:16 KJV)

THE RESURRECTION PROOFS

The Apostle Peter testified to the Holy Spirit's role in raising
Jesus from the grave.

For Christ also suffered once for sins, the righteous for
the unrighteous, to bring you to God. He was put to
death in the body but made alive in the Spirit. (1 Peter
3:18 NIV)

The change in the humanity of Jesus was apparent in that
He was able to ascend into Heaven that morning, perform His
High Priest duties and return to earth in time to walk with
those disciples on the road to Emmaus. He was able to rejoin
the other disciples afterward in a locked room. He could be
touched again, as He extended His hands and side as evidence of His suffering.

The writer to the Hebrews provided a description of the
atonement Jesus made as our High Priest in Hebrews Chapters 7-10. That will be reviewed later. Other scripture supports
the truth that Jesus was resurrected and how He appeared to
many as evidence that He was alive again. Paul wrote:

For what I received I passed on to you as of first importance: that Christ died for our sins according to the Scriptures, that he was buried, that he was raised on the third day according to the Scriptures, and that he appeared to Cephas, and then to the Twelve. After that, he appeared to more than five hundred of the brothers and sisters at the same time, most of whom are still living, though some have fallen asleep. Then he appeared to James, then to all the apostles, and last of all he appeared to me also, as to one abnormally born. (1 Corinthians 15:3-8 NIV)

John recorded his version of their last time with Jesus on earth in John Chapter 21. Jesus had more things to finish before He left the earth. He wanted the disciples to witness His resurrected body once more. He wanted to re-instate Peter to full time ministry before Pentecost. He wanted to leave him with a warning that suffering lay ahead. When Peter asked about John's future, He replied: "If I want him to remain until I return, what is that to you?" Only John recorded Peter's reconciliation, and Jesus' instructions for his future ministry:

When they had finished eating, Jesus said to Simon Peter, "Simon son of John, do you love me more than these?" "Yes, Lord," he said, "you know that I love you," Jesus said, "Feed my lambs." Again Jesus said, "Simon son of John, do you love me?" He answered, "Yes, Lord, you know that I love you." Jesus said, "Take care of my sheep." The third time he said to him, "Simon son of John, do you love me?" Peter was hurt because Jesus asked him the third time, "Do you love me?" He said, "Lord, you know all things; you know that I love you." Jesus said, "Feed my sheep. Very truly I tell you, when you were younger you dressed your-self and went where you wanted; but when you are old you will stretch out your hands, and someone else will dress you and lead you where you do not want to go." Jesus said this to indicate the kind of death by which Peter would glorify God. Then he said to him, "Follow me!" (John 21:15-19 NIV)

THE CUP OF GRATITUDE

This *cup* of Jesus' suffering we have been writing about is the *cup* we are asked to remember during Communion. Some call it the *Eucharist*, which in Greek implies that it is a wonderful gift of gratitude. May this serve as a reminder of all that Jesus did for us. We are told that:

When he had given thanks, he broke it and said, "This is my body, which is for you; do this in remembrance

FIGURE 1.1 *Communion still life* ©Magdalena Kucova/ShutterStock

of me." In the same way, after supper he took the cup, saying, "This cup is the new covenant in my blood; do this, whenever you drink it, in remembrance of me." For whenever you eat this bread and drink this cup, you proclaim the Lord's death until he comes. (1 Corinthians 11:24-26 NIV)

GUIDED DISCOVERY

Note: The word *Cup* appears 78 times in the Bible. It usually refers metaphorically to one's experience at a given time. A few examples from the Bible support that definition.

1. Write down the experience in each of these experiences from King David.

    a. Psalm 16:5

    b. Psalm 23:5

2. Jesus often used the word *cup* metaphorically to define a particular experience He was facing in the near future. Read the following verse and describe what you think He meant that applies to believers as well.

    a. Mark 10:35-40

3. What did you discover in this chapter about what Jesus meant by His use of the word in His toast at the Last Supper? (see Luke 22:20).

4. How did Jesus suffer mentally, beyond any physical suffering He experienced? How does that affect your feelings for Him?

5. Explain how Jesus used the Cup metaphor in Luke 22:39-42 to make a request of the Father on the Mount of Olives after supper. What did He model for us to follow?

6. According to the Apostle Paul, what did Jesus want us to do to keep in mind what He did for us, in mediating the New Covenant? (see 1 Corinthians 11:25).

7. From this chapter and Hebrews 9:11-15, what new discoveries did you find that relate to the Cup metaphor?

CHAPTER TWO

The New Covenant

The first phrase in the toast after the Last Supper is well understood. The *cup* definitely referred to the suffering that Jesus was going to face. According to Isaiah, the Father gave him a preview of the future. God was going to send His Son into humanity to fulfill His desire to regenerate those who were willing to accept His gift. The process would be different from keeping the Law. It would be something new. He would make a *new covenant* with all mankind.

At a pivotal time in the Old Testament, Isaiah prophesied God's Son coming to accomplish something new. Though He loved the Jews, God was not satisfied to relate only to them. He gave Isaiah this prophecy of His plan for Jesus:

I, the LORD, have called you in righteousness; I will take hold of your hand. I will keep you and will make you to be **a covenant for the people and a light for the Gentiles**, to open eyes that are blind, to free captives from prison and to release from the dungeon those who sit in darkness. "I am the LORD; that is my name! I will not yield my glory to another or my praise to idols. See, the former things have taken place, and new things I declare; before they spring into being I announce them to you." (Isaiah 42:6-9 NIV, Emphasis mine)

When the New Covenant was given to Jeremiah, it followed an introduction that would be the theme of the Gospel taught by Jesus:

"In those days people will no longer say, 'The parents have eaten sour grapes, and the children's teeth are set on edge.' Instead, everyone will die for their own sin; whoever eats sour grapes—their own teeth will be set on edge. "The days are coming," declares the LORD, "when **I will** make a new covenant with the people of Israel and with the people of Judah. It will not be like the covenant I made with their ancestors when I took them by the hand to lead them out of Egypt, because they broke my covenant, though I was husband to them," declares the LORD. "This is the covenant **I will** make with the people of Israel after that time," declares the LORD. "**I will** put my law in their minds and write it on their hearts. **I will** be their God, and they will be my people. No longer will they teach their neighbor, or say to one another, 'Know the LORD,' because they will all know me, from the least of them to the greatest," declares the LORD. "For **I will** forgive their wickedness and **will** remember their sins no more." (Jeremiah 31:29-34 NIV, Emphasis mine)

Notice the *I wills* that make it God's grace and not a conditional covenant. It was written for the nation of Israel. Jesus offered the new covenant to them, but they rejected it. The new covenant was God's answer to the prayers of men like David, Daniel and Jeremiah, as we will see later.

At the time of the Last Supper, Jesus had been witnessing to Israel for nearly three years. He performed miracles, healed the sick, called the dead back to life and fed thousands with a few loaves of bread and fish. He had acquired a band of disciples who were astonished at all that He had done. He had proven to them He was a man from God. They could not believe that He was going to die on a cross within a few hours. While they were in the upper room, He taught them the great truths recorded in John Chapters 13-16.

After supper, He raised his cup of wine and began to teach them some deeper truths about why He had been sent to the earth. He associated His cup of suffering with the words he called a *new covenant*. Jesus was referring to the prophecy revealed to Jeremiah. He would be the mediator of a new covenant for the people. The disciples had no idea what He meant.

The shock today is that most people still know very little about the New Covenant or its importance. The Jews did not want to give up living under the Law. Many people today are happy with their lifestyles and are not looking for any changes. A need exists to pick up the torch again and become more familiar with God's true covenant of grace. Time is running out and the light is growing dimmer and harder to find. We need to learn the truth from God's word in order to understand this covenant of grace that Jesus was introducing to His disciples.

THE MEANING OF THE NEW COVENANT

Jesus was not stating His rights or His last will and testament that night. He was providing the means by which the Father was going to create a new nature in humans through faith and the indwelling of the Holy Spirit. That was something totally new, as the rest of the toast would demonstrate. What did Jesus mean by a new covenant? Most dictionaries today call a covenant an agreement between parties regarding some formal action. Early translators of the Hebrew Bible into koine Greek chose the word *diatheke* to translate Jeremiah 31:31-34. It was understood to mean a covenant or promises between two or more people. When Jerome translated the old Greek Bible into Latin, he chose the word *testamentum* to replace the word *covenant*. What had been called the old covenant became the old testament. He confused the meaning of covenant promises between individuals with testaments of a person's last will and disposal of personal belongings.

The early Hebrew word for covenant was *berift*, pronounced *ber-eeth*. There were two types of covenants: those that were conditional and mutually binding and those that were gracious and unconditional, bound only by the one making the covenant and the other choosing to accept it. That was the new covenant Jesus was introducing at the Last Supper.

Unconditional covenants were made by God in the form of promises that He would fulfill, and the key phrase was *I will*. It was the key phrase in the case of the covenants given to Abraham in Genesis 12:1 and to king David in 2 Samuel Chapter 7. They all begin with *I will*:

"When your days are over and you rest with your ancestors, **I will** raise up your offspring to succeed you, your own flesh and blood, and **I will** establish his kingdom. He is the one who will build a house for my Name, and **I will** establish the throne of his kingdom forever. **I will** be his father, and he will be my son. **I will** punish him with a rod wielded by men, with floggings inflicted by human hands, But **my love will** never be taken away from him, as I took it away from Saul, whom I removed from before you. **Your house and your**

kingdom will endure forever before me; your throne will be established forever." (2 Samuel 7:12-16 NIV, Emphasis mine)

The ten commandments given to Moses were of a different nature. They had to be followed if Israel were to have a relationship with God. They were conditional, but not a set of rules by which one could earn rewards. The type of covenant made between God and Israel on the Exodus at Sinai was a conditional covenant of a righteous relationship:

"'You yourselves have seen what I did to Egypt, and how I carried you on eagles' wings and brought you to myself. Now if you obey me fully and keep **my covenant**, then out of all nations you will be my treasured possession. Although the whole earth is mine, you will be for me a kingdom of priests and a holy nation.' These are the words you are to speak to the Israelites." (Exodus 19:4-6 NIV, Emphasis mine)

When Moses delivered the above words to them, the people all promised to do everything the Lord had demanded (see Exodus 19:8). The weakness in that agreement was the failure of the people to keep their promise of the old covenant. With that background, an explanation may be found for not calling covenants a will or testament. The words old covenant and new covenant would appear to be more appropriate.

In Exodus Chapter 21, the Lord changed the rest of the old covenant to laws. "These are the laws you are to set before them." They were conditional and had judgments attached for failures. Once they were put in written form, and the people had affirmed they would abide by the rules, Moses performed the role of mediator between the people and God (see Exodus 24:7-8). He took the blood of animals and said: "This is the blood of the covenant that the Lord has made with you in accordance with these words." He was referring to the covenant being made that the people would abide by the Law. That was a perfect example of a conditional form of a covenant. The new one Jesus was introducing was full of grace and love. It required only the act of being willing to receive it by faith. With that history as an introduction, one is better prepared to search for a greater understanding of Jesus' meaning at the Last Supper when He said, "This cup is the new covenant."

THE PURPOSE OF THE NEW COVENANT

The promise of the New Covenant was, "I will put My law in their minds and write it on their hearts." Jesus introduced the purpose of this new covenant in His first teaching with the Pharisee, Nicodemus. The need was to create new natures in men and women that had been corrupted by Adam's fall.

Jesus introduced the necessity with this comment about the need to be born of the Spirit:

> "Very truly I tell you, no one can see the kingdom of God unless they are born again." "How can someone be born when they are old?" Nicodemus asked. "Surely they cannot enter a second time into their mother's womb to be born!" Jesus answered, "Very truly I tell you, no one can enter the kingdom of God unless they are born of water and the Spirit. Flesh gives birth to flesh, but the Spirit gives birth to spirit. You should not be surprised at my saying, 'You must be born again.'" (John 3:3-7 NIV)

The new birth was not understood. The things Jesus said were a preview of that which would be accomplished once the new promises were applied on the Day of Pentecost. Believers would not only have new natures, they would become children of God. When Jesus said, "This cup is the new covenant in My blood," He was referring to the fact that He was about to mediate the new covenant with His own blood. He was introducing the greatest act of love ever revealed to man. God was enabling Jesus to take the sins of the world upon Himself, along with freeing them from the condemnation of the old covenant.

When Israel began to crumble from within and outside from the Roman Empire, Jesus came to His own people with the good news of regeneration and freedom, called the New Covenant. After three years of ministry, the leaders and the self righteous rejected God's offer (see John 1:11-12). When His offer of forgiveness was ignored, it was apparent that there would be no reconciliation with Israel or Gentiles until new minds and new hearts were created through faith in Christ by the Holy Spirit. This change was necessary if God were to have the new family He desired.

God had a plan in which He was going to place His righteousness in the minds of those willing to receive His gift. He covenanted to replace their hardened hearts with a tender and loving heart in the image of Christ. Israel as a whole was unwilling as many people are today to surrender their will and ego to God. The evidence of having a new nature is the surrender of the self to God.

The magnitude of God's grace can be seen in the way He presented the new words and outline to Jeremiah. He explained to the prophet Ezekiel how He was going to do it in a way unheard of before in human history:

I will give you a new heart and put a new spirit in you;
I will remove from you your heart of stone and give
you a heart of flesh. I will put my Spirit in you and

move you to follow my decrees and be careful to keep my laws. (Ezekiel 36:26-27 NIV)

Something new had been added, "I will put my Spirit in you and motivate you." John recorded the words of Jesus years later in describing such a new heart:

"As the Father has loved me, so have I loved you. Now remain in my love. If you keep my commands, you will remain in my love, just as I have kept my Father's commands and remain in his love. I have told you this so that my joy may be in you and that your joy may be complete. My command is this, Love each other as I have loved you. Greater love has no one than this: to lay down one's life for one's friends." (John 15:9-13 NIV)

Central to the expression of that kind of selfless love was the presence of the promised Holy Spirit, who would be abiding in every believer. Before they left the upper room, Jesus prayed for that new nature:

"Father, just as you are in me and I am in you. May they also be in us so that the world may believe that you have sent me. I have given them the glory that you gave me, that they may be one as we are one—I in them and you in me—so that they may be brought to complete unity. Then the world will know that you sent me and have loved them even as you have loved me." (John 17:21-23 NIV)

It must be understood that the unity Jesus was praying for was that all believers have a oneness of being united in the body of Christ. That prayer was answered for all His followers on the Day of Pentecost.

When Jesus said, "This cup is the new covenant," He was confirming the emergence of a new covenant for His people. The covenant itself had a twofold purpose. It was offered to Israel as a redemptive gift to reconcile them to God's grace after all they had experienced in Babylon and Assyria (Jeremiah Chapters 30-31). It was intended to create righteous natures in all of God's fallen people, including the Gentiles. Israel, as a nation, refused it and turned on their Messiah.

That last night, Jesus knew that He was about to demonstrate the extent of God's love for all believers; for those who want to be with Him in eternity. The promise from the Father was that He was going to send the Holy Spirit to indwell believers with a new heart and mind that is in the image of Christ.

COMPETENT MINISTERS OF THE NEW COVENANT

A Pharisee called Saul was a living example of how God would bring about new natures in men and women. In his old nature, Saul, soon to be renamed Paul, wanted to hunt down and destroy those who opposed the teaching of the Pharisees. Jesus met him on the road to Damascus and gave him a new life and a new name. He called him to become a minister to the Gentiles. It was in that calling that he wrote these passages:

> He has made us competent as ministers of a new covenant—not of the letter but of the Spirit; for the letter kills, but the Spirit gives life. (2 Corinthians 3:6 NIV)

The change in the nature of believers would reconcile **even Gentiles** to God:

> Therefore, if anyone is in Christ, the new creation has come: the old has gone, the new is here! All this is from God, who reconciled us to himself through Christ and gave us the ministry of reconciliation: that **God was reconciling the world to himself in Christ, not counting people's sins against them**…. (2 Corinthians 5:17-19 NIV, Emphasis mine)

There is a promise of total forgiveness from sin in the New Covenant. How could anyone forget or ignore such a gracious forgiveness?

The Apostle Paul described a sevenfold unity that Jesus had prayed for as having been fulfilled in his letter to the church at Ephesus:

> There is **one body** and **one Spirit**, just as you were called to **one hope** when you were called; **one Lord, one faith, one baptism; one God and Father** of all, who is over all and through all and in all. (Ephesians 4:4-6 NIV, Emphasis mine)

This covenant could be called a *before-time covenant* in which each member of the Godhead had agreed to assume a role in restoring man to the status required to become a child of God. More evidence of that covenant will be seen in the following:

> Paul, a servant of God and an apostle of Jesus Christ to further the faith of God's elect and their knowledge of the truth that leads to godliness in the hope of eternal life, which God, who does not lie, **promised before the beginning of time,** and which now at his appointed season has brought to light through the preaching

entrusted to me by the command of God our Savior," (Titus 1:1-3 NIV, Emphasis mine)

But when the kindness and love of God our Savior appeared, he saved us, not because of righteous things we had done, but because of his mercy. He saved us through **the washing of rebirth** and **renewal by the Holy Spirit**, whom he poured out on us generously through Jesus Christ our Savior, so that, **having been justified by his grace, we might be heirs having the hope of eternal life**." (Titus 3:4-7 NIV, Emphasis mine)

The final promises mentioned in the New Covenant were that God would write His righteousness in the minds and hearts of those who place their faith in Christ. For nearly two centuries, the body of believers believed in and supported the New Covenant by word of mouth. With the exception of letters written to churches and the scrolls containing the words of the prophets, the people were dependent on the words and teaching of the disciples and apostles.

Think of where we would be today if Paul had not written his letters and influenced others like the writer of Hebrews and the great works of his friend Luke. Peter and John kept the truth alive with their writings. Our understanding of the New Covenant would have been very difficult without them.

The writer to the Hebrews explained that the new covenant was replacing the old:

"This is the covenant I will establish with the people of Israel after that time, declares the Lord. I will put my laws in their minds and write them on their hearts. I will be their God, and they will be my people. No longer will they teach their neighbor, or say to one another, 'Know the Lord,' because they will all know me, from the least of them to the greatest. For I will forgive their wickedness and will remember their sins no more." By calling this covenant "new," he has made the first one obsolete; and what is obsolete and outdated will soon disappear. (Hebrews 8:10-13 NIV)

The New Covenant brought light to the things that had been *mysteries* in the past: the new birth by the indwelling of the Holy Spirit, a new family called the church, and the forgiving and forgetting of sins. The new relationship with God would be a personal one.

GUIDED DISCOVERY

Note: The second phrase in the toast was the Title of a New
Covenant. It appeared first in Jeremiah 31:31-34, and meant to
be a comfort to Israel after 70 years of Captivity in Babylon.
The leaders of the Nation of Israel refused to accept it and Jesus
as well, except for a few.

1. Read some amazing prophecies given to Isaiah, describ-
    ing certain aspects of the New Covenant and the role
    that Jesus would play in introducing it. What parts of
    this prophecy do you find in the New Covenant?

    a. Isaiah 42:6-9

2. What are some of the differences you see immediate-
    ly between the Law, or Old Covenant, and the New?
    Give some illustrations.

3. From this chapter, what were some reasons the New
    Covenant slipped into oblivion for so many?

4. Explain the difference between a conditional covenant and an unconditional one. Illustrate.

5. Jesus introduced the opening truths of the New Covenant to an inquiring Pharisee named Nicodemus. What was the great change introduced to him in John 3:3-7?

6. What was lost by Adam and Eve that is regenerated under the New Covenant? (see Hebrews 8:10-13).

7. Share some benefits we have, thanks to the experiences and writings of the Apostle Paul after his conversion. What did he pass on to Titus, one of his own disciples? (see Titus 3:48).

8. Describe some mysteries explained at the end of this chapter.

CHAPTER THREE

In My Blood

When Jesus added the words *in my blood* at the Last Supper, He was using old covenant terms for removing sin (see Leviticus 16). Two male goats were selected. One was chosen to give its blood for the sacrifice and the other was to be used as the scapegoat who took away the sins of those who had sinned. The Lord's application was related to His dual role in removing and forgiving our sins, so the last two promises of the new covenant could be applied to us, "I will forgive their sins and remember them no more."

When He reached the age of 30 years, Jesus began His earthly ministry. In John 1:29, the Baptizer pointed Him out to his own disciples when he saw Him passing by, saying: "Look, the Lamb of God, who takes away the sin of the world." The phrase was known to the Jews as the *azazel*, or the scapegoat, in the Law for the atonement of sins. There were two animals involved. One was selected to provide blood for the sacrifice and the other was used as an agent to carry the forgiven sins of the sinner out into the desert. When the time came, Jesus would provide both the blood of the atonement, and assume the role of the redeemer who took sins upon Himself and died for them. As usual, the old covenant (Law) set the pattern, but the new covenant was superior in that it did not have to be repeated. The next time you read the book of Revelation, note how often the resurrected Jesus is called *The Lamb*. That was His High Priest role on earth.

The value of the new covenant, being associated with the blood of Jesus, is seen in three major acts of God's grace related to the forgiving and removing of sin: (a) a superior reconciliation, (b) a ransom for sin and (c) a removal of the memory of our sins. The old covenant set the pattern, but was inferior to the power of the new. The new, using the blood of Christ, replaced the blood of animals in that His blood produced a greater sacrifice. The grace of a better reconciliation is central to this chapter for the same reason when applied to the value of His life. The grace of a prepared ransom to free individuals from sin is presented in more detail in Chapter Four. The propitiation value of Christ's life to satisfy the justice of God is covered in Chapter Five.

A SUPERIOR RECONCILIATION

The word *reconciliation* has been selected to replace the word *mediation*, as it is more relevant to the new covenant of grace than the Law covenant that no one could keep. The writer of the book of Hebrews recorded several sections in his book on the principle of reconciling God and man in the new covenant. He introduced the reason God wanted His Son to be the reconciler. Jesus was fully human and fully God in one person. He was perfect, for He had never sinned. He was willing, after some anguish, to become sin so believers might be forgiven:

> The former regulation is set aside because it was weak and useless (for the Law made nothing perfect), and a better hope is introduced, by which we draw near to God. And it was not without an oath! Others became priests without any oath, but he became a priest with an oath when God said to him: "The Lord has sworn and will not change his mind: 'You are a priest forever.'" Because of this oath, Jesus has become the guarantor of a better covenant. Now there have been many of those priests, since death prevented them from continuing in office; but because Jesus lives forever, he has a permanent priesthood.

> Therefore he is able to save completely those who come to God through him, because he always lives to intercede for them. Such a high priest truly meets our need— one who is holy, blameless, pure, set apart from sinners, exalted above the heavens. Unlike the other high priests, he does not need to offer sacrifices day after day,

THE CUP AND THE COVENANT

first for his own sins, and then for the sins of the people.
He sacrificed for their sins once for all when he offered
himself. For the law appoints as high priests men in all
their weakness; but the oath, which came after the law,
appointed the Son, who has been made perfect forever.
(Hebrews 7:18-28 NIV)

The writer of the book of Hebrews was well-versed in the
Law and customs of his own people. He knew the changes
God was making. In his own understanding, he knew the
benefit of God choosing His own Son to reconcile the gap between His holiness and the wicked natures of man. Jesus had
taught and healed enough to cause anyone to see that He was
who He said He was. The religious leaders rejected Him and
God's offer of grace. They preferred living under the Law, as
they saw it. It became evident to Jesus at the Last Supper that
it had to be done the Father's way. His will determined the
decision Christ made later that night on the Mount of Olives,
when He resigned Himself to die on the cross:

Therefore, when Christ came into the world, he said:
"Sacrifice and offering you did not desire, but a body
you prepared for me; with burnt offerings and sin offerings you were not pleased. Then I said, 'Here I am—
it is written about me in the scroll—I have come to do

your will, my God.'" First he said, "Sacrifices and offerings, burnt offerings and sin offerings you did not desire, nor were you pleased with them"—though they were offered in accordance with the law. Then he said, "Here I am, I have come to do your will." He sets aside the first to establish the second. And by that will, we have been made holy through the sacrifice of the body of Jesus Christ once for all. (Hebrews 10:5-10 NIV)

The last line summed it up for Jesus. He chose to take the sins of man on Himself and pour out His life on the cross as a ransom to reconcile man to God. In Hebrews 10:10, the answer is given: "We have been made holy by and through the sacrifice of the body of Christ once for all." There was more to take place on the Day of Pentecost: "But now in Christ Jesus you who once were far away have been brought near by the blood of Christ." (Ephesians 2:13 NIV).

A RANSOM FOR SIN

In the past, when the old covenant high priest had finished applying the blood, he returned to the *azazel,* or scapegoat, and placed both of his hands on the goat's head imputing the sins and rebellions of Israel onto the goat to be carried away into the desert. Jesus carried our sins away by taking them upon Himself and carrying them onto the cross. He bore our sins and shed His blood to ransom us from the condemnation of sin through faith in His dying for us. This is the way He carried our sins away; He took them upon Himself and carried them away in the morning resurrection. He was resurrected from the grave in a new spiritual body (see John 20:17).

It should be noted that John the Baptist had seen Jesus only as a forgiver of sin and not as a substitute, but like the sacrificial lamb of God of the old covenant. When officials quizzed him about why he was baptizing, John said his goal in offering baptisms was for repentance and to reveal Jesus as Messiah. He was given that opportunity when Jesus approached him. The anointing of the Lord's baptism in Matthew 3:13-17 officially set Jesus apart as a High Priest in the likeness of Melchizedek.

When the Baptizer first hesitated to baptize Him, Jesus said: "It is proper for us to do this to fulfill all righteousness." It was necessary to anoint Jesus as a high priest as God desired. On the third day after the cross, He arose to perform a priestly role in Heaven. He had paid the ransom for sinners by giving His life on the cross. His next duty in Heaven was to deliver His precious blood as a final atonement. That, too, was covered in Hebrews. On the morning He arose, He was thirty years old, the age required to be a priest under the Law. He was resurrected to life with a spiritual body, ready to become a High Priest:

Day after day every priest stands and performs his religious duties; again and again he offers the same sacrifices, which can never take away sins. But when this priest had offered for all time one sacrifice for sins, he sat down at the right hand of God, and since that time he waits for his enemies to be made his footstool. For by one sacrifice he has made perfect forever those who are being made holy. (Hebrews 10:11-14 NIV)

Much is made of the fact that Jesus was ordained by the Father to be a priest after the order of Melchizedek. This man was a priest/king from Salem. He came forth to bless Abraham for his obedience to God. He appears first in Genesis 14:18-20. He was a prototype of the kind of high priest God wanted His Son to be, a priest/king. That is His present role in Heaven. He intercedes for believers before the Father. Like Melchizedek, Jesus will be the eternal king one day, promised to the Jews.

A FINAL REMOVAL OF OUR SIN RECORD (FORGIVENESS)
In the introduction of his letter to a Hebrew audience, the writer refers to: "God speaking to our forefathers through the prophets and recently through the authority of His Son." The author, in the main theme of his letter to the Jews, attested that Jesus was the Son of God, reflecting an exact image of

God's grace while He was on earth. He explained that Jesus was provided as a purification of sins before He returned to sit at the right hand of the Father in Heaven. That was His ultimate act as our high priest. In that one act, He defeated the desires of Satan to see God's people under condemnation. Jesus paid the price for forgiveness for all who believe Him (see 1 John 2:2 and Genesis 3:15).

After supporting the authority of Jesus to serve as our high priest, the author gave several reasons for the superiority of the New Covenant. The old had served its purpose. God in His grace had spoken through prophets like Isaiah, Jeremiah and Ezekiel that He was creating a new covenant with a new priesthood that would be eternal. He added that it was necessary for the Law to be abolished as a means of making one righteous in their human nature. It was never intended to do that. No one had been able to keep the Law, except Jesus.

One benefit of Jesus as our high priest is that He is eternal and continues to represent us in Heaven. Another fact is that He did not need to be offering sacrifices over and over. He sacrificed for our sins, once for all, by taking His own blood into the Holy of Holies in Heaven.

A major feature of the atonement Jesus made was that it was a *propitiation* atonement (that is an English word that was used to translate the Greek word *hilasmos*, meaning mercy and appeasement). There was a difference in the meaning of that kind of atonement by Jesus, for His blood was of such value it was capable of *satisfying*, not just *appeasing*, the justice of God (see Romans 3:25).

The Supremacy of His Blood

The last two promises of the New Covenant were about the forgiveness of our sins and God's promise to remember them no more. Only the supremacy of Christ's blood was capable of such a sacrifice. The letter to the Colossians opened with that understanding applied to all aspects of our lives:

> And he is the head of the body, the church; he is the beginning and the firstborn from among the dead, so that in everything he might have the supremacy. For God was pleased to have all his fullness dwell in him, and through him **to reconcile to himself all things, whether things on earth or things in heaven, by making peace through his blood, shed on the cross.** Once you were alienated from God and were enemies in your minds because of your evil behavior. **But now he has reconciled you by Christ's physical body through death to present you holy in his sight**... (Colossians 1:18-22 NIV, Emphasis mine)

Isaiah Chapter 53 contained the same message, saying only the sacrifice of the Son would satisfy God's perfect justice in order to extend grace:

After he has suffered, he will see and be satisfied; by his knowledge my righteous servant will justify many, and he will bear their iniquities. (Isaiah 53:11 NIV)

That power was attested to by Paul, by the writer to the Hebrews, by Peter and by John. The same values were taught by each one.

Paul wrote to the Ephesian Church: "But now in Christ Jesus you who once were far away have been brought near by the blood of Christ." (Ephesians 2:13).

The writer to the Hebrews witnessed:

How much more, then, will the blood of Christ, who through the eternal Spirit offered himself unblemished to God, cleanse our consciences from acts that lead to death, so that we may serve the living God! (Hebrews 9:14 NIV)

The Apostle Peter had the same truth:

Who have been chosen according to the foreknowledge of God the Father, through the sanctifying work of the

Spirit, obedience to Jesus Christ and sprinkled with his blood: Grace and peace be yours in abundance...with the precious blood of Christ, a lamb without blemish or defect. (1 Peter 1:2,19 NIV)

John also referred to the power of the blood of Christ in his introduction to Revelation:

Jesus Christ, who is the faithful witness, **the firstborn from the dead**, and the ruler of the kings of the earth. To him who loves us and has **freed us from our sins by his blood**. (Revelation 1:5 NIV, Emphasis mine)

The satisfaction of God's Justice was given to Paul:

But now apart from the law the righteousness of God has been made known, to which the Law and the Prophets testify. This righteousness is given through faith in Jesus Christ to all who believe. There is no difference between Jew and Gentile, for all have sinned and fall short of the glory of God, and all are justified freely by his grace through the redemption that came by Christ Jesus. God presented Christ as a sacrifice of atonement through the shedding of his blood—to be received by faith... (Romans 3:21-25 NIV)

The new grace would be that through faith in Christ's blood, God has placed righteousness in the hearts and minds of believers with a new covenant: "Salvation is found in no one else, for there is no other name under heaven given to mankind by which we must be saved." (Acts 4:12).

IN MEMORY OF THE LAST SUPPER

FIGURE 3.1 *Eucharist* ©Jonathunder via Wikimedia Commons/Public Domain

This scene, like so many others like it, help us remember the Cup metaphor, the Covenant recorded in the Word of God, and the blood so valuable it only had to offered once to satisfy the justice of God. We are asked by our leaders to say, "Thank you Lord Jesus!"

Guided Discovery

Note: The old covenant contained all the rites and rituals involved in covering sins with an expiation atonement of animal blood, periodically placed on the Mercy Seat in the Holy of Holies room of the Tabernacle on the Exodus. The atonement Jesus made was once for all (see 1 John 2:2).

1. In the old covenant, two animals were used to atone. How did Jesus fulfill both roles, in His once-for-all atonement?

2. What was it that was so much superior in the sacrifice Jesus made?

3. In what way are the two verses of 1 John 2:2 and Genesis 3:15 connected?

4. What was Jesus able to do in His role as our High Priest that the old covenant high priest could not do?

5. Explain the difference between the old and the new covenants regarding the righteousness of God. What made the difference?

6. When Jesus died on the cross, the heavy curtain leading into the Holy of Holies was torn in two from top to bottom. What was the significance of that for believers today?

7. What did Jesus say to Mary Magdalene on the morning of His resurrection in John 20:10-17?

8. Read Hebrews 10:11-14 and explain in how many ways Jesus was superior as our High Priest.

CHAPTER FOUR

Poured Out for You

Jesus used the words *poured out for you* as the last phrase of His covenant toast. It would be natural to interpret the words as an extension of the phrase that preceded it, *in my blood*. His blood was necessary to meet the need for a propitiation atonement, but the *poured out for you* referred to another purpose. Jesus had been sent to give His life as a ransom to redeem us from the condemnation of the Law. Support for that interpretation is found in the Greek word *ekxunno-menon*. The first part of it means *to pour or gush out*. The *gushing out* referred to the reaction of the spear thrust into His side to prove He was dead:

> But when they came to Jesus and found that he was already dead, they did not break his legs. Instead, one of the soldiers pierced Jesus' side with a spear, bringing a sudden flow of blood and water. The man who saw

it has given testimony, and his testimony is true. He knows that he tells the truth, and he testifies so that you also may believe. (John 19:33-35 NIV)

No subject in the Bible is given more attention than the death of God's Son. The value of His life was sufficient to pay the ransom. His suffering was God's grace in providing His Son as a substitute to satisfy His justice. The metaphor for ransom was the phrase *poured out for you*. It was paid for on the cross. To support these truths, a cross section of biblical verses will follow in the outline of this chapter: (a) a foreordained death, (b) for redemption and (c) resurrection proofs to aid faith. It was God's design that Jesus was to suffer, die and take away our sin. Mentally, Jesus suffered by knowing what lay ahead of him. He predicted His future treatment at the hands of the chief priests and teachers of the Law. He also knew the manner in which He would die. This is the evidence that God's design for our salvation was foreordained.

FOREORDAINED DEATH FOR REDEMPTION

Three different times He warned the disciples that He would soon die as a substitute for many. The first time was just after He had asked Peter, "Whom do you say I am?" He described their faith in Him as the foundation upon which He was going to build a Church. He knew they had become believers. On their way back to Jerusalem, a year before He was to die, He revealed more to them.

After they had returned to Galilee, Jesus took Peter and the sons of Zebedee with Him to witness His transfiguration. While they were on the mountain, they heard a voice from a cloud say, "This is my Son, whom I love; with him I am well pleased. Listen to Him." After that amazing experience, they headed back to Galilee with the rest of the disciples. There Jesus made His second prediction:

When they came together in Galilee, he said to them, "The Son of Man is going to be delivered into the hands of men. They will kill him, and on the third day he will be raised to life." And the disciples were filled with grief. (Matthew 17:22-23 NIV)

Another prediction occurred as Jesus and His disciples were heading back to Jerusalem for the last time:

Now Jesus was going up to Jerusalem. On the way, he took the Twelve aside and said to them, "We are going up to Jerusalem, and the Son of Man will be delivered over to the chief priests and the teachers of the law. They will condemn him to death and will hand him over to the Gentiles to be mocked and flogged and crucified.

On the third day he will be raised to life!" (Matthew 20:17-19 NIV)

The disciples understood few specifics of His death being a vicarious substitution until Paul became an apostle. John's gospel was the exception:

Christ died for the ungodly…while we were yet sinners, Christ died for us. (Romans 5:6,7 NIV)

Christ…gave himself up for us as a fragrant offering and sacrifice to God. (Ephesians 5:2 NIV)

He…delivered him up for us all… (Romans 8:32 KJV)

For Christ also suffered once for sins, the righteous for the unrighteous,… (1 Peter 3:18 NIV)

"I am the living bread that came down from heaven. Whoever eats this bread will live forever. This bread is my flesh, which I will give for the life of the world." (John 6:51 NIV)

His life became **a ransom** to free us from bondage to sin and the Law.

For this reason Christ is the mediator of a new covenant, that those who are called may receive the promised eternal inheritance—now that he has died as **a ransom** to set them free from the sins committed under the first covenant. (Hebrews 9:15 NIV, Emphasis mine)

"'No person devoted to destruction may be ransomed; they are to be put to death." (Leviticus 27:29 NIV)

Once Jesus was declared dead, His life became the **ransom** paid to redeem believers. The last part of the Greek phrase *poured out* refers to a dispensing of something. Note that it says *"for you"* and not *"on you."* If the word was *on you*, it would mean conferring a covenant, as Moses did on the Exodus. Jesus was referring to the pouring out of His life *for you* as an act of ransom that would redeem believers from condemnation under the Law.

The Apostle Paul confirmed believers as being *redeemed* from the curse of the Law:

Christ **redeemed** us from the curse of the law by becoming a curse for us, for it is written: "Cursed is everyone who is hung on a pole." He **redeemed** us in order that the blessing given to Abraham might come to the Gentiles through Christ Jesus, so that by faith we might receive the promise of the Spirit. (Galatians 3:13-14, Emphasis mine)

God foreordained that Jesus complete two more purposes in order to fulfill the new covenant. He had to make an atonement and He had to support faith in His resurrection. The atonement will be addressed in Chapter Five.

RESURRECTION PROOFS FOR STRENGTHENING FAITH

The belief in a life after death came very late in Israel's history. One example was the lingering disbelief among Sadducees. The Pharisees, like Gamaliel and Paul who believed in a resurrection, created a split within the Sanhedrin. One of the earliest in the Old Testament to believe was Job. The progression of his faith is apparent in these ancient passages:

"If only you would hide me in the grave and conceal me till your anger has passed! If only you would set me a time and then remember me! If someone dies, will they live again? All the days of my hard service I will wait for my renewal to come. You will call and I will answer you; you will long for the creature your hands have made." (Job 14:13-15 NIV)

"Oh, that my words were recorded, that they were written on a scroll, that they were inscribed with an iron tool on lead, or engraved in rock forever! I know that my redeemer lives, and that in the end he will stand on the earth. And after my skin has been destroyed, yet in my flesh I will see God; I myself will see him with my own eyes—I, and not another. How my heart yearns within me!" (Job 19:23-27 NIV)

Jesus had taught the disciples that He would arise from the grave on the third day several times, but they found it hard to believe:

"Behold, we are going up to Jerusalem, and the Son of Man will be delivered to the chief priests and the scribes; and they will condemn Him to death and will hand Him over to the Gentiles. They will mock Him and spit on Him, and scourge Him and kill Him, and three days later He will rise again." (Mark 10:33-34 NASB)

One more example of their confusion was on the morning of His resurrection. The disciples had a hard time believing the tomb was open and empty. Later in the day, Jesus joined two followers on their way to a nearby town called Emmaus. He asked them why they were so sad for they had not recognized

Him as He followed. They replied that they had hoped Jesus was the Messiah, but He had been crucified. They even told how some of the women had found the tomb empty. Jesus said:

"How foolish you are, and how slow to believe all that the prophets have spoken! Did not the Messiah have to suffer these things and then enter his glory?" (Luke 24:25-26 NIV)

Jesus left them after they recognized him and began to reveal Himself to others. He started with the apostles who were gathered in a locked upper room. He entered without knocking revealing that His spiritual body was not restrained by solid matter. In addition to this startling appearance was another resurrected feature of His spiritual body. It had healed already but the scars were still visible in His hands and side. Thomas was not there and said he would not believe until he saw and touched Jesus himself. A week later, Jesus entered the locked room while Thomas was there:

Then he said to Thomas, "Put your finger here; see my hands. Reach out your hand and put it into my side. Stop doubting and believe." Thomas said to him, "My Lord and my God!" Then Jesus told him, "Because you have seen me, you have believed; blessed are those who have not seen and yet have believed." (John 20:27-29 NIV)

The Apostle John ended his gospel with these words:

Jesus performed many other signs in the presence of his disciples, which are not recorded in this book. But these are written that you may believe that Jesus is the Messiah, the Son of God, and that by believing you may have life in his name. (John 20:30 NIV)

Jesus revealed more resurrection proofs to the Apostle Paul after his conversion, for he had information that could only have come from Jesus. He used that information to establish what became known as the apostolic view of our resurrected bodies. He passed it on to the churches he visited, and taught it to the young ministers he trained. Examples will be given at the end of this chapter.

The Apostle John gathered more insight to add to what Paul received about our resurrected bodies that must be reviewed before we leave the subject. They were recorded in his epistles and the Revelation. Another part of the life of the resurrected Jesus was the assumption of His role as our high priest on the morning of His resurrection. It will be covered in Chapter Five.

CONCLUSIONS

We know from the promise to the thief on the cross that the moment we die, our souls go to be with Christ in the present Paradise. What we do know and believe is that in the end of our lives we will be like Jesus:

> Dear friends, now **we** are children of God, and what **we will be** has not yet **been** made known. But **we** know that when Christ appears we shall **be like him**, for **we** shall see **him** as he is. (1 John 3:2 NIV, Emphasis mine)

The apostles believed at the end of their lives or they would not have followed Him into martyrdom.

> For what I received I passed on to you as of first importance: that Christ died for our sins according to the Scriptures, that he was buried, that he was raised on the third day according to the Scriptures, and that he appeared to Peter and then to the Twelve. After that, he appeared to more than five hundred of the brothers and sisters at the same time, most of whom are still living, though some have fallen asleep. Then he appeared to James, then to all the apostles, and last of all he appeared to me also, as to one abnormally born. (1 Corinthians 15:3-8 NIV)

But Christ has indeed been raised from the dead, the first-fruits of those who have fallen asleep...Christ, the firstfruits; then, when he comes, those who belong to him. Then the end will come. For as in Adam all die, so in Christ all will be made alive. But each in turn: he hands over the kingdom to God the Father after he has destroyed all dominion, authority and power. (1 Corinthians 15:20; 23-24)

Because we know that the one who raised the Lord Jesus from the dead will also raise us with Jesus and present us and you to himself. (2 Corinthians 4:14 NIV)

"My Father's house has many rooms; if that were not so, would I have told you that I am going there to prepare a place for you? And if I go and prepare a place for you, I will come back and take you to be with me that you also may be where I am. You know the way to the place where I am going." (John 14:2-4 NIV)

If Jesus was not raised from the grave, why didn't the Jews refute it? Only seven weeks later, Peter preached the resurrection of Jesus and hundreds believed. What changed the doubtful disciples into committed men?

GUIDED DISCOVERY

Note: The words *poured out for you* appeared to be related to the blood of Jesus as a sacrifice. Instead, we discover it was related to a proof He was dead.

1. Psalm 34:20 had always been seen as related to the Messiah. When the guards broke the legs of the other two and did not bother to break the legs of Jesus, it was seen as a fulfillment of prophecy. How was the "gushing out" even more significant in fulfilling a need in the New Covenant?

2. In what way was His dying more valuable than His shed blood?

3. Read the promises of the New Covenant and share the one you believe was powerful enough to erase the memory of sins in a believer.

4. Give some reasons you have for Jesus making so many public appearances after His resurrection.

5. What means most to you about the resurrection of Jesus? Explain.

6. Righteousness was attributed for obeying the Law. What is the reward for placing your faith in Christ's death for you? Give a verse.

CHAPTER FIVE

Mediating the New Covenant

One of the purposes for writing this book was to find answers as to why there has been such a lack of teaching and preaching on the subject of the New Covenant. The subject of this chapter may be one of the answers. The resurrection of Christ and the New Covenant are of necessity totally dependent upon one another. Because of that relationship, a wide gap has developed between the doctrinal beliefs of churches concerning covenants.

Jesus referred to Satan as the prince of this world (see John 14:30). He has used the disagreement, *as to which covenant gave birth to the church*, to split the theologians and the churches they influence. If the church began with the covenant with Abraham, the resurrection and the New Covenant are less significant. If the Church Christ called *My Church* began at Pentecost, the resurrection and the New Covenant are given the attention that the Word of God suggests. This chapter will focus on three areas of relevance based on the Scriptures: (a) supporting the need for Christ's resurrection, (b) supporting the need for His priesthood and (c) supporting the need for a New Covenant of righteousness.

SCRIPTURAL SUPPORT FOR THE RESURRECTION

The supports begin with the Lord's own teaching about His resurrection. He gave His disciples a prediction of His future resurrection right after He announced His plan to build a new covenant church of His own:

> From that time on Jesus began to explain to his disciples that he must go to Jerusalem and suffer many things at the hands of the elders, the chief priests and the teachers of the law, and **that he must be killed and on the third day be raised to life**. Peter took him aside and began to rebuke him. "Never, Lord!" he said. "This shall never happen to you!" (Matthew 16:21-22 NIV, Emphasis mine)

The next comment about His future came soon after their witnessing the Lord's transfiguration. The disciples were beginning to pay more attention:

As they were coming down the mountain, Jesus gave them orders not to tell anyone what they had seen until the Son of Man had risen from the dead. They kept the matter to themselves, discussing what "rising from the dead" meant. (Mark 9:9-10 NIV)

At the beginning of His final visit to Jerusalem and the Last Supper, Jesus brought up the subject again. They began to be more convinced, although they were still not aware of why He had to die:

Now Jesus was going up to Jerusalem. On the way, he took the Twelve aside and said to them, "We are going up to Jerusalem, and the Son of Man will be delivered over to the chief priests and the teachers of the law. They will condemn him to death and will hand him over to the Gentiles to be mocked and flogged and crucified. On the third day he will be raised to life!"(Matthew 20:17-19 NIV)

The death and resurrection must have been at the forefront of His mind all the time. Although the comments He made had little effect at the time, the seeds were sown in their minds. After the cross all the predictions were recalled, strengthening their faiths. The predictions have the same effects in our minds that the resurrection appearances had. All that was missing at the time was, "Why was it necessary that the Messiah die and be raised from the grave?" The question is answered in this next segment.

SCRIPTURAL SUPPORT OF THE NEED FOR A GREATER HIGH PRIEST

The New Covenant Jesus referenced to and the blood that was shed for a propitiation atonement, required a more powerful high priest. The scriptures supporting such a view are found in the inspired writing of the book of Hebrews:

> But because Jesus lives forever, he has a permanent priesthood. Therefore he is able to save completely those who come to God through him, because he always lives to intercede for them. (Hebrews 7:24-25 NIV)

The definition of a mediator is one that serves as a go-between in the finalizing of a covenant. On the Exodus, Moses took the blood of a lamb and sprinkled some of it on the altar and sprinkled the rest on the people to confirm the conditions of the Old Covenant. The use of animal blood offered from the people through a priest was a sign of commitment on behalf of the people and a sign of acceptance from God. It would mediate a covenant between the two parties. In the mediation of the New Covenant, the blood of Jesus was of a dual nature. It represented the commitment of the Father to keep His promises, and it represented a cleansing of the people to whom the promises were made:

> How much more, then, will the blood of Christ, who through the eternal Spirit offered himself unblemished to God, cleanse our consciences from acts that lead to death, so that we may serve the living God! For this reason Christ is the mediator of a new covenant, that those who are called may receive the promised eternal inheritance—now that he has died as a ransom to set them free from the sins committed under the first covenant. (Hebrews 9:14-15 NIV)

To perform a mediation of the New Covenant, a new kind of High Priest was needed. He had to die, provide the blood, be resurrected, make a once-for-all atonement in order to mediate a better covenant and enter into heaven as our High Priest. His emergence as a priest began with a prophecy made in Psalm 110:4 by King David. It was quoted as a statement from God in the manner of an oath. Regarding His Son: "The Lord has sworn and will not change His mind. You are a priest forever, in the order of Melchizedek."

Melchizedek appeared suddenly in scripture as a priest/ king out of Salem, whose name meant *king of righteousness* and *king of peace*. He met Abraham in that role as Abraham was returning with all the plunder he had gained while rescuing his nephew Lot from raiding warlords. Abraham generously gave the priest a tenth of all he had gained. The priest/king was a perfect model to describe Jesus for he did not base his priesthood on ancestry, nor according to custom.

He was known as a king priest honored because of the power of who He was. Unlike the other priests in the Old Testament, Jesus was assigned a permanent priesthood by the Father that will last forever at His right hand. All of this is mere background, for that was only an example of His new role. What follows is even more astounding as to all He was able to perform as the mediator of God's New Covenant. He had a resurrected body that could ascend and descend.

The Law was not designed to make men righteous. Therefore, God had chosen to create a new covenant of a higher order. The New Covenant was designed to regenerate new minds and hearts in believers. A high priest was needed that would have more flexibility. Since God was offering a new covenant of grace, a change had to take place in the priesthood.

God's eternal High Priest would be required to replace the blood of animals with His own blood to cleanse man from sin, to the extent that God would be able to extend grace rather than judgment. Being both fully God and fully human, Jesus had the power to represent God to man and man to God in the mediation. That was something no other priest could do.

He was capable of giving His life as a ransom and redemption from sin. He would be able to make an eternal atonement with unlimited power to create a new spiritual birth through the Holy Spirit. Because of a new birth, He and the Father could live within believers. Only the Son of God could meet those requirements.

Support for a Regeneration of Righteousness

The New Covenant was to begin on the Day of Pentecost with the coming of the Holy Spirit. In those fifty days from the cross, (a) God raised Jesus from the grave to make the eternal atonement and (b) provided Him time to reveal His victory over death with personal appearances. All the things that took place after the cross and His resurrection was recorded in the book of Acts, when He appeared before His disciples. Ten days before Pentecost, Jesus told them that He must return to Heaven so He and the Father could return with the Holy Spirit:

> After his suffering, he presented himself to them and gave many convincing proofs that he was alive. He appeared to them over a period of forty days and spoke about the kingdom of God. On one occasion, while he

was eating with them, he gave them this command: **"Do not leave Jerusalem, but wait for the gift my Father promised**, which you have heard me speak about. For John baptized with water, but in a few days you will be baptized with the Holy Spirit." (Acts 1:3-5 NIV, Emphasis mine)

In order to preserve the account of the power of the atonement Jesus made, Paul was inspired to write later in Romans the effect of the atonement:

God presented Christ as a sacrifice of atonement, through the shedding of his blood—to be received by faith. He did this to demonstrate his righteousness, because **in his forbearance** he had left the sins committed beforehand unpunished—he did it to demonstrate his righteousness at the present time, so as to be just and the one who justifies those who have faith in Jesus. (Romans 3:25-26 NIV, Emphasis mine)

With His justice fully satisfied, God was able to express the grace necessary to fulfill the New Covenant in the lives of believers. They did not understand, but a great change was about to take place. God's righteousness, satisfied with the atonement of Jesus, was free to use the Holy Spirit to place

His righteousness within believers. He was going to answer Christ's prayer by living within us spiritually, creating a new family out of believers until Jesus returns. All was ready to fulfill the promises of His New Covenant, even toward those in the past.

To complete the understanding of justification made possible by the atonement of Christ, a new review is needed of what Paul meant when he added the word *forbearance* in Romans 3:25. He was referring to some in the past who had served God but had committed sins that could be forgiven now, after the atonement by Jesus was able to satisfy the justice of God.

Abraham, Moses, King David, Daniel and Israel provide evidence of God's grace made possible for repentant believers of the past by the atonement of Christ. The word repentance was vital to understand why their sins were not judged until the death of Christ. In some cases, the Law called for their death. Those in the past, who confessed their sins and asked for forgiveness, could be declared free of their condemnation under the Law.

David was given insight into his need for a righteous new mind and new heart that could only be generated by the Holy Spirit. God had allowed David and Daniel to request such forgiveness before an answer was ever given to Jeremiah to write the New Covenant.

DAVID'S SIN:
TRANSGRESSION OF "YOU SHALL NOT COMMIT ADULTERY"

> For I know my transgression, and **my sin is always before me**. Against you, you only, have I sinned and done what is evil in your sight; so you are right in your verdict and justified when you judge. Surely **I was sinful at birth, sinful from the time my mother conceived me**. (Psalm 51: 3-5 NIV, Emphasis mine)

He asked for a new heart and new spirit that would be willing to obey. It was almost as if he knew in advance of the New Covenant promises:

> Create in me a pure heart, O God, and renew a steadfast spirit within me. Do not cast me from your presence or take your Holy Spirit from me. Restore to me the joy of your salvation and grant me a willing spirit, to sustain me. (Psalms 51:10-12 NIV)

DANIEL AND ISRAEL'S TRANSGRESSIONS (DANIEL 9:4)

Daniel was aware of the promises of the New Covenant because he had read Jeremiah. On the basis of the promised New Covenant, he prayed for forgiveness of the transgressions of Israel and himself. He began by saying that it was through the writings of Jeremiah that he was reminded that Israel's seventy years of punishment and the transgression of the people of God was about to end. Those words were written by Jeremiah in Chapters 29-30, just before the great passage in the next chapter, introducing the promises of the New Covenant.

The introductory words of Daniel Chapter 9 may have created a hope for himself and Israel that led to his great prayer of repentance. It is printed partially here in respect of its great humility:

I prayed to the LORD my God and confessed and said, "Alas, O Lord, the great and awesome God, who keeps His covenant and lovingkindness for those who love Him and keep His commandments, we have sinned, committed iniquity, acted wickedly and rebelled, even turning aside from Your commandments and ordinances. Moreover, we have not listened to Your servants the prophets, who spoke in Your name to our kings, our princes, our fathers and all the people of the land. "Righteousness belongs to You, O Lord, but to us open shame, as it is this day—to the men of Judah, the inhabitants of Jerusalem and all Israel, those who are nearby and those who are far away in all the countries to which You have driven them, because of their unfaithful deeds which they have committed against

You. Open shame belongs to us, O Lord, to our kings, our princes and our fathers, because we have sinned against You. To the Lord our God belong compassion and forgiveness, for we have rebelled against Him; nor have we obeyed the voice of the LORD our God, to walk in His teachings which He set before us through His servants the prophets. Indeed all Israel has transgressed Your law and turned aside, not obeying Your voice; so the curse has been poured out on us, along with the oath which is written in the law of Moses the servant of God, for we have sinned against Him." (Daniel 9:4-11 NASB)

"O my God, incline Your ear and hear! Open Your eyes and see our desolations and the city which is called by Your name; for we are not presenting our supplications before You on account of any merits of our own, but on account of Your great compassion. O Lord, hear! O Lord, forgive! O Lord, listen and take action! For Your own sake, O my God, do not delay, because Your city and Your people are called by Your name." (Daniel 9:18-19 NASB)

Before he had finished praying and confessing his sins and the sins of Israel, the angel Gabriel appeared, saying:

"O Daniel, I have now come forth to give you insight with understanding. At the beginning of your supplications the command was issued, and I have come to tell you, for you are highly esteemed; so give heed to the message and gain understanding of the vision." (Daniel 9:22-23 NASB)

THE SINS OF MOSES IN DISOBEYING GOD

Denied entrance into the promised land, the sin of Moses in disobeying God was to be forgiven under the grace of God. His last days were recorded in Deuteronomy Chapter 34:

Then the LORD said to him, "This is the land I promised on oath to Abraham, Isaac and Jacob when I said, 'I will give it to your descendants.' **I have let you see it with your eyes, but you will not cross over into it.**" And Moses the servant of the LORD died there in Moab, as the LORD had said. He buried him in Moab, in the valley opposite Beth Peor, but to this day no one knows where his grave is. Moses was a hundred and twenty years old when he died, yet his eyes were not weak nor his strength gone. The Israelites grieved for Moses in the plains of Moab thirty days, until the time of weeping and mourning was over. (Deuteronomy 34:4-8 NIV, Emphasis mine; cf. Deuteronomy 34:10-12)

Moses was denied access to the promise land while alive because of his sin of disobedience. In Luke 9:28, he was allowed spiritually to confirm Jesus' transfiguration, after his death, along with Elijah, on the mount. He was praised by God after his death and will be forgiven along with David and Daniel.

Before he died, Moses was directed to ascend Mount Nebo and get a glimpse of the Holy Land from a distance. Thanks to that last promise of the New Covenant, I believe Moses will enter into the millennial kingdom: *I will forgive their sins and remember them no more.*

When Jesus died on the cross, the huge curtain (before the entrance to the Holy of Holies in the Temple) was torn from top to bottom. It was God's way of saying that sinners would no longer need to go through a priest to confess their sins. God is available to receive prayer twenty-four hours a day. If you have a need or a concern that is heavy to bear alone, enter into His presence and pray. Since the way is open, set a special time each day to pray. When you pray, address your prayers to the Father and close them in the name of Jesus. He made it possible for you to have that connection, and the benefit of privacy in our prayers. "So I say to you: Ask and it will be given to you; seek and you will find; knock and the door will be opened to you. For everyone who asks receives." (Luke 11:9-10).

In the next chapter we will learn that the word *church* developed into more than one meaning. We will learn that the terms *Old* and *New Testaments* describing the sections of the Bible are not last wills and testaments. They are better described as The Old Covenant and The New Covenant. We will also learn the difference between an assembly of people who are called *Christians* and *The Body of Christ*. Jesus began approving plans for His church before he died. He laid the foundations for His church in the upper room discourse on the role of the Holy Spirit's baptism of regeneration. Insights into the dynamics of regeneration appear in the next chapter.

GUIDED DISCOVERY

Note: Three needs were met in mediating the New Covenant. Without them, there could be no New Covenant.

1. What was so important in this chapter about Christ's resurrection?

2. Who was Melchizedek, and how did he support the kind of High Priest Jesus would be?

3. What traits did Jesus have that made Him a better Mediator than Moses?

4. Some say the church was formed by the covenant given to Abraham. What shortcoming does that view have, in contrast with the Church being formed on the Day of Pentecost?

5. How was the teaching made to Nicodemus fulfilled on that same day? Explain.

6. What advantage was there in having the justice of God appeased rather than His wrath? (see Romans 3:22-26).

7. How do we experience the same baptism of the Holy Spirit that Jesus experienced? (Remember, He is the "first fruits" of a resurrection to a new life).

CHAPTER SIX

Birth of the Church

THE CHURCH PREDICTED BY JESUS

On the night of the Last Supper, Jesus predicted the upcoming birth of His Church. He warned the disciples that He was about to leave this life, but that He would return. He introduced the new involvement of the Holy Spirit by way of a promise found in the New Covenant: "I will put my laws in their minds and write them on their hearts." The things He described would come about through the experience of a baptism in the Spirit and fire on Pentecost. This would be the forming of the Church. The body of believers would continue the ministry until He returns to set up His kingdom.

Jesus also promised each believer would have help from the indwelling of His Spirit. The one command He was referring to was that we love one another as He and the Father had loved us. These verses have no meaning if the church is only an extension of the promises to Abraham about Israel. What a comfort they have been to believers who know they are members of God's new family:

> "If you love me, keep my commands. And I will ask the Father, and he will give you another advocate to help you and be with you forever—**the Spirit of truth**. The world cannot accept him, because it neither sees him nor knows him. But you know him, for he lives with you and will be in you. I will not leave you as orphans; I will come to you. Before long, the world will not see me anymore, but you will see me. Because I live, you also will live. On that day you will realize that I am in my Father, and you are in me, and I am in you.... Anyone who loves me will obey my teaching. My Father will love them, and we will come to them and make our home with them. Anyone who does not love me will not obey my teaching. These words you hear are not my own; they belong to the Father who sent me. All this I have spoken while still with you. But the Advocate, the Holy Spirit, whom the Father will send in my name, will teach you all things and will remind you of everything I have said to you." (John 14:15-20; 23-26 NIV, Emphasis mine)

Today, if the truths Jesus was teaching are not realized or understood, knowledge of Scripture is needed. For a variety of reasons, the teaching of truth about the power of the Holy Spirit in our lives has been blocked. When asked why there is no teaching or preaching about the Holy Spirit, the usual answer is "It is too controversial." The intent of this study is to remove that fear by staying with the words of Jesus. He cannot bear a false witness:

> While Apollos was at Corinth, Paul took the road through the interior and arrived at Ephesus. There he found some disciples and asked them, "Did you receive the Holy Spirit when you believed?" They answered, "No, we have not even heard that there is a Holy Spirit." So Paul asked, "Then what baptism did you receive?""John's baptism," they replied. Paul said, "John's baptism was a baptism of repentance. He told the people to believe in the one coming after him, that is, in Jesus." On hearing this, they were baptized in the name of the Lord Jesus. (Acts 19:1-5 NIV)

Many are in that position today. They have become believers in Jesus but do not know about the Spirit. Jesus gave Him names to describe His power within us. He is our Advocate, The Comforter, Our Counselor and The Spirit of Truth.

Until He came, there could be no Church.

JESUS LAID THE FOUNDATIONS FOR THE CHURCH

Before Jesus left the upper room with His disciples, He poured out His heart to the Father in a personal prayer. He asked Him to protect them and keep them; to set them apart by the truths that He had taught them. In John Chapter 17, He closed His prayer by asking God for **unity** within those who would come to believe in Him. He asked three different times that the Father would unite believers into a oneness the Trinity has. He closed with the words, "May the love you have for me be in them, and may I be in them as well."

When the Holy Spirit came, those requests became standards for the New Covenant kind of Church. From Scripture we learn that there was a list of foundational blocks on which Christ was to build His Church, with the help of the Spirit. He was the cornerstone. He used Peter to describe the foundation upon which He would build. He called it "faith":

And **I** tell you that you are Peter, and on this rock **I** will **build** my church, and the gates of Hades will not overcome it. (Matthew 16:18 NIV, Emphasis mine)

The Following have been Called the Building Blocks of Christ's Church:

a. **Faith.** That is the basis. Jesus validated that standard with His comment about a faith like Peter's. Christ being the cornerstone, Peter gave his total allegiance to follow Him. Jesus commended him saying:

> And I tell you that you are Peter, and on this rock I will **build** my church, and the gates of Hades will not overcome it. (Matthew 16:18 NIV, Emphasis mine)

b. **New Birth.** Equally important was the need to be *born again* through the baptism of the Holy Spirit, demonstrated for all to see on the Day of Pentecost.

> Just as a body…has many parts, but all its many parts form one body, so it is with Christ. **For we were all baptized by one** Spirit so as to form one body—whether Jews or Gentiles, slave or free—and we were all given the one Spirit to drink. (1 Corinthians 12:12-13 NIV, Emphasis mine)

c. **Unity.** The enemy has divided theologies, but not our inner unity.

> "My prayer is not for them alone. I pray also for those who will believe in me through their message, that all of them may be one, Father, just as you are in me and I am in you. May they also be in us so that the world may believe that you have sent me. I have given them the glory that you gave me, that they may be one as we are one I in them and you in me—so that they may be brought to complete unity." (John 17:20-23 NIV)

d. **Fellowship.** We are more than followers now. We are family.

> They devoted themselves to the apostles' teaching and to fellowship, to the breaking of bread and to prayer. Everyone was filled with awe at the many wonders and signs performed by the apostles. All the believers were together and had everything in common. They sold property and possessions to give to anyone who had need. Every day they continued to meet together in the temple courts. They broke bread in their homes

and ate together with glad and sincere hearts, praising God and enjoying the favor of all the people. The Lord added to their number daily those who were being saved. (Acts 2:42-47 NIV)

e. **Love** and **Hope.** These two attitudes round out our faith.

If I speak in the tongues of men or of angels, but do not have love, I am only a resounding gong or a clanging cymbal. If I have the gift of prophecy and can fathom all mysteries and all knowledge, and if I have a faith that can move mountains, but do not have love, I am nothing. And now these three remain: faith, hope and love. But the greatest of these is love. (1 Corinthians 13:1-2,13 NIV)

f. **Jesus is the Head.** This promise assures our future in the New Heaven.

And God placed all things under his feet and appointed him to be **head** over everything for the church, which is his **body**, the fullness of him who fills everything in every way. (Ephesians 1:22-23 NIV, Emphasis mine)

g. **Growth.** God did not want us to be without under-standing of His Word:

> So Christ himself gave the apostles, the proph-ets, the evangelists, the pastors and teachers, to equip his people for works of service, so that the body of Christ may **be built up** until we all reach unity in the faith and in the knowledge of the Son of God and become mature, attaining to the whole measure of the fullness of Christ. (Ephesians 4:11-13 NIV, Emphasis mine)

THE DAY OF PENTECOST AND THE BIRTHDAY OF THE CHURCH

The New Covenant was instituted ten days after Jesus re-turned to the Father. Jerusalem was filled with worshippers from all over the Roman Empire. They were gathered to cel-ebrate the Day of Pentecost. It had several meanings for Israel. It was a holiday set aside to enjoy the spring harvest; a day of thanksgiving for Moses and his mediation of the Old Cov-enant. It was a reminder of the fiftieth day after escaping from slavery in Egypt. Pentecost was still a day of thanksgiving for the Nation. The disciples, Mary (the mother of Jesus), other women and His brothers were gathered together in an upper room praying and waiting for the promise Jesus had made.

It happened early in the morning. As predicted, Jesus sent the Holy Spirit in a baptism of fire:

> Suddenly a sound like the blowing of a violent wind came from heaven and filled the whole house where they were sitting. They saw what seemed to be tongues of fire that separated and came to rest on each of them. **All of them were all filled with the Holy Spirit** and began to speak in other tongues as the Spirit enabled them. (Acts 2:2-4 NIV, Emphasis mine)

The birth of the Church was just like the baptism of fire predicted by John the Baptist. The Holy Spirit entered into people rather than just coming upon them. He did more than empower, He regenerated them into new beings:

> Now there were staying in Jerusalem God-fearing Jews from every nation under heaven. When they heard this sound, a crowd came together in bewilderment, because each one heard their own language being spoken. Utterly amazed, they asked: "Aren't all these who are speaking Galileans? Then how is it that each of us hears them in our native language? Parthians, Medes and Elamites; residents of Mesopotamia, Judea and Cappadocia, Pontus and Asia, Phrygia and Pamphylia, Egypt

and the parts of Libya near Cyrene; visitors from Rome (both Jews and converts to Judaism); Cretans and Arabs—we hear them declaring the wonders of God in our own tongues!" Amazed and perplexed, they asked one another, "What does this mean?" (Acts 2:5-12 NIV)

Examples of miraculous changes included the regenerated new nature and voice of Peter addressing the crowd that day. He stood up and faced them. He began by referring to them as "Fellow Jews and all of you who live in Jerusalem, allow me to explain this to you." To the insinuations that the disciples might be intoxicated, he chose to point out that it was only nine o'clock in the morning. He told them this happening was the fulfillment of a prophecy from Joel, the prophet. All the promises Jesus had made about the new natures being provided by the Holy Spirit for His disciples were being fulfilled. He quoted Joel, "I will pour out my Spirit on that day and people will prophesy." (Joel 2:28).

That got their attention by connecting the prophecy with the miracles and signs God had used to introduce Jesus as His Son. Peter said that God handed Jesus over to the rulers, according to His foreknowledge and purpose, so that they, with the help of wicked men, could crucify Him. At that point the crowd called out, "What shall we do?" Peter answered, with the help of the Holy Spirit, that they should follow his advice:

"Repent and be baptized, every one of you, in the name of Jesus Christ for the forgiveness of your sins. **And you will receive the gift of the Holy Spirit.** The promise is for you and your children and for all who are far off— for all whom the Lord our God will call." With many other words he warned them; and he pleaded with them, "Save yourselves from this corrupt generation." **Those who accepted his message were baptized, and about three thousand were added to their number that day.** (Acts 2:38-41 NIV, Emphasis mine)

The Church of Jesus Christ was born that day!

A SUPERIOR PRIESTHOOD

The Church that Christ referred to as His body had to have a different priesthood:

If perfection could have been attained through the Levitical priesthood—and indeed the law given to the people established that priesthood—why was there still need for another priest to come, one in the order of Melchizedek, not in the order of Aaron? For when the priesthood is changed, the law must be changed also. He of whom these things are said belonged to a differ-ent tribe, and no one from that tribe has ever served at the altar. For it is clear that our Lord descended from Judah, and in regard to that tribe Moses said nothing about priests. And what we have said is even more clear if another priest like Melchizedek appears, one who has become a priest not on the basis of a regulation as to his ancestry but on the basis of the power of an indestructible life. (Hebrews 7:11-16 NIV)

The new covenant church had to have a superior high priest to make atonement, and live eternally making intercession for believers in heaven:

Unlike the other high priests, he does not need to offer sacrifices day after day, first for his own sins, and then for the sins of the people. He sacrificed for their sins once for all when he offered himself. (Hebrews 7:27 NIV)

THE NEW COVENANT BODY OF A BELIEVER
WAS TO BE A TEMPLE

In the past, Israel was required to go to the Temple for worship. The Church of Jesus Christ was able to worship wherever two or three were gathered in His name. Jesus spoke these words about His love and commitment to those who follow Him. "For where two or three gather in my name, there am I with them." (Matthew 18:20).

Paul, the Apostle, wanted the Corinthians to be that kind of church as he wrote:

Do you not know that your bodies are temples of the Holy Spirit, who is in you, whom you have received from God? You are not your own; you were bought at a price. Therefore honor God with your bodies. (1 Corinthians 6:19-20 NIV)

All believers are baptized with the power of the Holy Spirit the moment they believe. From the beginning, that union resulted in believers being regenerated by the Holy Spirit into a family that God could call His own. During the balance of that first century, a history of the early church is found in the book of Acts. Two forms of the church were listed: those that were described as singular, or a local church (like the church at Jerusalem, Antioch and Ephesus), and later, as the churches multiplied, they were described in a larger, or more collective sense (with plural names like the Galatians, Macedonians and the Romans). God is most pleased with what is in the heart of individuals, not in the size or numbers in the congregation. The early church in Jerusalem was local and unique in the design Jesus had given to the disciples.

CONCLUSION

The Church Christ set up was designed to be independent of the nation of Israel. The loss of any faith in a millennial kingdom for the Jews may have been planted in the minds of some who believe falsely that God has rejected them forever. There were changes, however. Circumcision was no longer required. The Law was replaced by a new nature through the indwelling of the Holy Spirit. The priesthood was changed. The Jewish Temple and its worship center was destroyed within the next thirty five years. The training of the disciples enabled them to become teachers and expositors of church doctrine, as seen in the lives of Peter, John, Philip, James and Paul. The church was scattered by persecution, but not before establishing a set of standards advocated by Jesus. He had given the disciples instructions on how to evangelize and promised to empower them with the Spirit. He told Peter he would be given keys to the kingdom of heaven with guidance as how to lead. It became evident on the Day of Pentecost.

In the first century history of the church, it was believed that the true church was created on that Day of Pentecost. The view was changed when the Roman Church viewed its existence as an extension of the *ekklesia* of Israel. For that reason, they saw the origin of the church as beginning with the covenant made with Abraham. Neglected by many were the mysteries revealed to Paul regarding the New Covenant and the Church. The Church that Jesus made came through faith and a new birth. The view that God was finished with Israel was as false as them saying the Church had to embrace circumcision. Toward the end of his ministry, the apostle Paul chose to teach what God had revealed to him (see Chapter Ten). This was a revelation to him how God was going to use the Church, through grace, to restore Jews back to "God Himself":

> I do not want you to be ignorant of this mystery, brothers and sisters, so that you may not be conceited: Israel has experienced a hardening in part until the full number of the Gentiles has come in, and in this way all Israel will be saved. As it is written: "The deliverer will come from Zion; he will turn godlessness away from Jacob. **And this is my covenant** with them when I take away their sins." As far as the gospel is concerned, they are enemies for your sake; but as far as election is concerned, they are loved on account of the patriarchs, for God's gifts and his call are irrevocable. (Romans 11:25-29 NIV, Emphasis mine)

Church standards set by Christ were designed to produce mature believers in spiritual growth and witnessing to others about Jesus. It was the reason for so much emphasis on sound teaching, and for increasing in the knowledge of the Word of

God—the Bible. Paul was aware of his responsibility to the churches. In Romans 10:17 he said, "Faith comes from hearing the message, and the message is heard through the word about Christ." God's desire for all of us, in becoming a part of His church, is to love His Son and to love one another. He wants us to become mature in our faith, especially during times of suffering. Jesus asked that of His disciples just before He died:

> "Therefore go and make disciples of all nations, baptizing them in the name of the Father and of the Son and of the Holy Spirit, and teaching them to obey everything I have commanded you. And surely I am with you always, to the very end of the age." (Matthew 28:19-20 NIV)

The prophecy in Matthew was directed toward the disciples operating out of the new Church. The Isaiah prophecy was for those whose focus was still anchored in the past:

> You have heard these things; look at them all. Will you not admit them? "From now on I will tell you of new things, of hidden things unknown to you. They are created now, and not long ago; you have not heard of them before today. So you cannot say, 'Yes, I knew of them.'" (Isaiah 48:6-7 NIV)

Guided Discovery

Note: John the Baptist said, "I baptize with water. But one more powerful than I will come. He will baptize you with the Holy Spirit and with fire." (Luke 3:16).

1. What did Jesus teach His disciples about the birth of His Church at the Last Supper? (see John 14:15-26).

2. Describe what happened on the Day of Pentecost, when the Church Christ promised was given birth (see Acts 2:1-12).

3. How did Jesus say the first two promises of the New Covenant would be fulfilled? How did He describe it to Nicodemus in John 3:3-5?

4. The new births of believers was compared to a baptism in which believers are baptized, through faith, into Christ's death and to be raised like His resurrection. Explain the metaphor in your own words after reading Romans 6:1-5.

5. How would it help born again Christians, who are not aware that the Holy Spirit lives within them, to read this chapter?

6. Read the last part of the Lord's prayer after the Last Supper, and share the unity He prayed for in all believers (see John 17:20-26). Do you believe the Father answered that prayer? If so, how does that affect your faith?

7. If you are a "building block" in Christ's Church, you have that list within you. Of all the attributes listed, which one means most to you? Explain why.

CHAPTER SEVEN

The Proofs
of a New Creation

The days after the death of Christ and His resurrection were like the days and nights of England during World War II. As Winston Churchill said, "Never in the field of human conflict was so much owed by so many to so few." That same saying could be applied to the disciples and the number that came to believe on the Day of Pentecost. The world was under condemnation and Judaism had helped kill their Messiah. The coming of Christ and His disciples were like the RAF keeping London from being destroyed. The persecution against the new creation, after the coming of the Holy Spirit, was led by a young Pharisee called Saul. He was determined to destroy what he thought was a threat to his nation. Where would Christianity be today if men like Stephen, and others like him among the disciples, had not given their lives to support their faith in Christ?

CHRIST'S PRAYER FOR BELIEVERS

The prelude to this section of our study is found in John Chapter 17:11-26. It has been called the Lord's High Priestly Prayer for believers. If the church began with the Covenant of Abraham, why would Jesus pray this prayer?

> And now I am no more in the world, but these are in the world, and I come to thee. Holy Father, keep through thine own name those whom thou hast given me, that they may be one, as we are. While I was with them in the world, I kept them in thy name: those that thou gave me I have kept, and none of them is lost, but the son of perdition; that the scripture might be fulfilled. And now come I to thee; and these things I speak in the world, that they might have my joy fulfilled in themselves. I have given them thy word; and the world hath hated them, because they are not of the world, even as I am not of the world. I pray not that thou should take them out of the world, but that you should keep them from the evil. They are not of the world, even as I am not of the world. Sanctify them through thy truth: thy word is truth. As you have sent me into the world, even so have I also sent them into the world. And for their sakes I sanctify myself, that they also might be sanctified through the truth. Neither

pray I for these alone, but for them also which shall believe on me through their word; **That they all may be one**; as thou, Father, art in me, and I in thee, **that they also may be one in us**: that the world may believe that you have sent me. And the glory which you gave me I have given them; **that they may be one, even as we are one: I in them, and thou in me, that they may be made perfect in one**; and that the world may know that you have sent me, and have loved them, as you have loved me. Father, I will that they also, whom thou hast given me, be with me where I am; that they may behold my glory, which you have given me: for you loved me before the foundation of the world. O righteous Father, the world hath not known thee: but I have known thee, and these have known that you have sent me. And I have declared unto them thy name, and will declare it: that the love wherewith you have loved me may be in them, and I in them. (John 17:11-26 KJV, Emphasis mine)

Jesus made three requests that believers be made *one as we are one*. At the end, He defined the requests as a *complete unity*. What did He mean by that? Paul answered that in His letter to the Ephesians:

There is one body and one Spirit, just as you were called to one hope when you were called; one Lord, one faith, one baptism; one God and Father of all, who is over all and through all. (Ephesians 4:4-6 NIV)

It would help everyone to read that prayer before reading what took place next in the lives of the disciples—and our own lives—as a result of that prayer. He was asking the Father to create and protect His new family after He was gone, whose future would be with Him in eternity. We can be assured that the Father answered His Son in the special requests He made after the Last Supper. Jesus had forty days after His resurrection and the time of His departure to return to the Father and the Spirit. He planned to return with them on the Day of Pentecost, to indwell believers. Jesus had strengthened faith in Him with His resurrection and various appearances. That is what caused all the disciples to be in Jerusalem as requested. The day was important in their history for another reason.

On the Day of Pentecost in the Old Testament, Moses had mediated the old covenant on the Exodus with the sprinkled blood of animals (see Exodus 24:7-8). On the same day centuries later, a new covenant was being offered to anyone who was willing to receive it by faith in Christ. The new creation would occur as a result of being baptized into a new birth, through the indwelling power of the Holy Spirit, as a result of faith. In John 3:3 Jesus told Nicodemus, "No one can see the kingdom of God without being born again." What other proof do we have that the church came into being on the Day of Pentecost?

Many proofs have been suggested as to why no former Church could have existed before Pentecost that satisfied the justice of God. The following are all supported by Scripture:

1. The death of Christ was needed to redeem man from condemnation under the old covenant.

2. His resurrection and ascension was necessary to make an atonement to satisfy God's justice.

3. Only the indwelling of the Holy Spirit could create a new birth with righteous natures.

4. A Church called the body of Christ was needed that united Jews and Gentiles by faith alone under a new covenant.

5. The New Covenant Church fulfilled prophecy.

6. Only the "new creation" united both Jews and Gentiles into one body.

7. Only the New Covenant church provided a permanent priesthood.

Added to the above list was: (a) the desire of God to give Jeremiah a prophecy of a New Covenant of Grace (Jeremiah 31:31-34) and (b) the testimony of all the disciples concerning the presence of the Church which was credible.

On the Day of Pentecost, there was visible evidence of a new nature of righteousness in Peter, as he stood to answer those who thought the disciples had been drinking. It was remarkable how God used him and these former fishermen to spread the *good news*, or *gospel*, at that point in history. The change in Peter on the Day of Pentecost was like a new man had been born. He had a new *mind* and a new *heart*. He was no longer a braggart or one who pulled back under pressure. He became the "Billy Graham" of his day when he addressed the crowd in Jerusalem. On that day he encouraged the large crowd of Jewish and Gentile souls into a faith in Christ, causing each one to become a new creation for the Father. Peter, the fisherman who had become a Bible teacher, began to quote a psalm of King David to them as a part of that message:

Lord, you alone are my portion and my cup; you make my lot secure. The boundary lines have fallen for me in

pleasant places, surely I have a delightful inheritance.
I will praise the LORD, who counsels me; even at night
my heart instructs me. I keep my eyes always on the
LORD. With him at my right hand, I will not be shaken.
Therefore my heart is glad and my tongue rejoices; my
body also will rest secure, because you will not abandon me to the realm of the dead, nor will you let your
faithful one to see decay. (Psalm 16:5-10 NIV)

Peter applied this well-known passage to his audience as
a message from David in his prophecy. He saw this as being
a fulfillment of the covenant that the Father had made with
David that one of his descendants would be raised from the
dead to rule on his throne. The audience was prepared in their
memories and hopes for that one to come. So, when Peter mentioned that Israel had been responsible for the death, burial,
and resurrection of Jesus who was Lord and Messiah, many
people were heart-broken. The New Covenant was made
available to the world from that day forward. The Father had
answered the Son's prayer for a family. He also included all of
us who believe:

They devoted themselves to the apostles' teaching and
to fellowship, to the breaking of bread and to prayer.
Everyone was filled with awe at the many wonders and

signs performed by the apostles. All the believers were together and had everything in common. They sold property and possessions to give to anyone who had need. Every day they continued to meet together in the temple courts. They broke bread in their homes and ate together with glad and sincere hearts, praising God and enjoying the favor of all the people. And the Lord added to their number daily those who were being saved. (Acts 2:42-47 NIV)

After the large crowds had left Jerusalem, Peter and John continued going to the Temple to pray. One day a crippled beggar saw them and asked for money. Peter responded by asking him to pay attention to what he was about to say. Peter said, "Silver and gold, I do not have, but what I do have I give to you." Taking the man's hand, Peter said, "In the name of Jesus Christ of Nazareth, walk." After they helped the man to his feet, his feet and ankles suddenly became strong and he began to walk on his own. When he entered the Temple with Peter and John, jumping and praising God, people recognized him as the beggar and were filled with awe and wonder as to what had happened to him.

When people began to gather around them, Peter had another audience. He said: "Men of Israel, why does this surprise you?" He asked them, "Why did they stare and act as if it were by his own power or godliness that made the man walk?" Peter used the opportunity to give the gospel to the crowd. He confronted them first with the fact that they had disowned Jesus and had given Him over to Pilate. He said, "You had Him killed, but God raised Him from the dead, of which we are witnesses."

As Peter was encouraging the people to repent and worship Jesus, some priests and the captain of the Temple guard came by. They put Peter and John in jail overnight. Their reward was that many who had heard them turned to Christ in faith, bringing the number of believers to about five thousand. Fearing a response from the crowds, the leaders released Peter and John with a warning to stop preaching about Jesus. Peter and John had the answer, "Which is right in God's eyes: to listen to you, or to him? You be the judges! As for us, we cannot help speaking about what we have seen and heard." (Acts 4:19-20).

The family members of Abraham were imputed with righteousness. The new family of born again believers in Christ are made righteous as sons and daughters of God. The apostles and other believers were one in their faith as the persecutions increased. Finally, they had to appoint seven godly men as deacons to tend the widows, the poor and the aged. One of the men selected was called Stephen. He was full of God's grace and power that was seen and heard by the men who arrested

Peter and John. They acquired some false witnesses who said they had heard the man utter words of blasphemy against Moses and God. When asked by the Sanhedrin if the charges were true, Stephen gave the history of the Jews and fearlessly accused the leaders as murderers of Jesus. Witnesses said his face was like that of an angel as he spoke.

The leaders grabbed him as he was speaking, dragged him out of the city and began to stone him. They placed their coats at the feet of a man called Saul. With his last words, the young man prayed, "Lord, do not hold this sin against them." Luke then wrote words that must have hurt him to write about a friend, "Saul was there giving his approval Stephen's death." (see Acts 7:58).

The event scattered all believers from Jerusalem, except for the disciples. Later that same year, the young Pharisee called Saul of Tarsus was converted. He was the man at whose feet the men laid their clothing while stoning Stephen. His name was changed to Paul after a dramatic conversion to Christ on the way to Damascus Syria.

CREATING AN APOSTLE TO THE GENTILES

Saul had continued persecuting believers in Christ, until one day on the road to Damascus he was struck blind by a great flash of light from heaven. When he fell to the ground, he heard a voice speaking to him, "Saul, Saul, why do you persecute me?" He thought it had to be from God, for he said strangely, "Who are you Lord?" Jesus identified Himself and told Saul, "Get up on your feet and go into the city where you will be told what to do." (see Acts 9:3-6).

Those selected to deal with Saul were alarmed until Jesus told them He had selected him to be a vessel to carry His name to the Gentiles and their kings. A man called Ananias obeyed and went to the house where Saul had been taken. He did as he was told and placed his hands on Saul. He told him that Jesus had sent him so he might see again and be filled with the Holy Spirit. When the scales fell from his eyes and he could see again, Saul got up and was baptized. After witnessing for a few days in Synagogues in Damascus, the Jews set out to kill him. The followers of Jesus hid Saul and lowered him down one of the city walls to escape. Jesus led him into Arabia for three years where he was given new insights as to what God was doing. He wrote about his instruction in his epistle to the Galatians:

> I did not go up to Jerusalem to see those who were apostles before I was, but I went into Arabia. Later I returned to Damascus. Then after three years, I went up to Jerusalem to get acquainted with Cephas (Peter) and stayed with him fifteen days. (Galatians 1:17-18 NIV, Clarification mine)

Saul, the Pharisee, was divinely selected and converted to be the dominant teacher and missionary for the New Covenant church. In Galatians 1:12-13, he was taken aside to Arabia and taught personally by Jesus Himself. He was given two specific mysteries from God to reveal to the world. The next chapter will focus more on his new role as an apostle to the Gentiles.

Saul became known as Paul, Apostle to the Gentiles, while Peter was to serve as the Apostle to the Jews. Each in his own way served the Lord greatly in the roles given to them. Paul became a great teacher of the deep truths given to him by Jesus.

THE CHURCH WAS SCATTERED AND ENLARGED

The church expanded as far as Antioch in present day Turkey after the death of Stephen. A great number of people believed and the disciples were first referred to as Christians in Antioch Syria. At first they only took the message to Jews. Some from other areas began to witness to the Greeks. When the church at Jerusalem heard about the growth in Antioch Syria, they sent Barnabas to meet Paul and form a missionary team. They ministered there for over a year when they were told to prepare for their first missionary journey. The timing would have been around 45-49 AD. Luke described how the church laid hands on them and commissioned them as church missionaries. He outlined their entire journey and experience in Acts Chapters 12-14. They were set on their way with a blessing and a prayer for protection by the Holy Spirit. In an aside, Luke mentioned that they had taken young John Mark with them as a helper.

The trio sailed to the isle of Cyprus and entered a Jewish synagogue in Salamis, before crossing to Paphos where a Roman pro-consul was interested in hearing the word of God. Two of the pro-consul's attendants were unbelievers who tried to break up the conversation. Paul turned to the one known as a sorcerer and put a curse on him to blind him temporarily. It so impressed Sergius Paulus, the proconsul, he became a believer.

Paul and his companions sailed to Perga and the mainland where the young John Mark may have become homesick. Or he may have reacted to Paul's boldness and decided to return home. Luke began to change the way he referred to the pair of missionaries. He began to call them Paul and Barnabas instead of Barnabas and Paul from that point on in Scripture. The message that Paul gave was very much like the one he had heard Stephen use before he was stoned. Gentiles were attentive but the Jews were infuriated. When John Mark decided to go home, Paul was offended and upset he had left. Barnabas defended him. The two of them visited four more places, including Antioch Psidia in Asia Minor and then south to Iconium, Lystra and Derbe in Galatia, before returning to Antioch in Turkey. They spoke and many Gentiles turned to Christ. Paul and Barnabas returned from their first mission with good news about the openness of the Gentiles. Some of Christian Jews wanted the new Gentile converts to be circumcised. The first church council was called to be held in Jerusalem to deal with some of the issues related to how strict they should be with Gentile converts. Peter was asked to speak.

In Acts 15:6, Peter shared his experience of seeing the coming of the Holy Spirit and His indwelling of uncircumcised Gentiles in the home of Cornelius. He and the six witnesses all saw the same signs to verify their new natures. Peter asked, "Who was I that I should oppose God?" After Peter explained the Gentiles had been baptized, the council praised God's grace and agreed that God had granted even the Gentiles repentance unto life. James, the brother of Christ and head of the church in Jerusalem, made a judgment to extend grace to the Gentiles and sent them a letter confirming the openness of the local council to Gentile converts. It was at that point Paul began to write to the churches where he had ministered. The Lord had given him the truths to write down for believers of the future in those letters. He laid the doctrinal foundations of the true New Covenant Church.

GUIDED DISCOVERY

Note: Review the list of proofs why no other church could have existed before Pentecost that would have satisfied the righteousness and justice of God.

1. Explain how the testimony, or lives, of the disciples provide credibility that they saw the resurrected Christ, and believed in Him and His words.

2. Was there any change in Peter after Pentecost? How would you account for such a rapid change?

3. What evidence do we have that Saul died to his old nature and was made new, after his experience on the road to Damascus?

4. What changed in the grace of God toward the follow-
    ing, once His Son died on the cross? Describe in your
    own words.

    a. Gentiles (Like Cornelius)

    b. Believing Jews (Like the Disciples)

    c. Past Sins not judged (David, Moses and Aaron)

5. Jesus said He would come back soon. Was He referring
    to Pentecost? If so, how? (see John 17:20-26).

6. Who was head of the first Church council in Jerusalem?
    What did Paul and Peter add to their conclusion regard-
    ing Gentiles?

7. Read Paul's first letter to Thessalonica and describe what
    he wrote about Jesus.

CHAPTER EIGHT

The Dynamics of Faith

O ne of the first distinctions about Paul's gospel messages was that he was not teaching something man-made. He had not received it from any man, nor was he taught by anyone other than Jesus Himself (see Galatians 1:11). He reviewed his past history in Judaism and his animosity toward believers as evidence that he previously had no knowledge of the true gospel of Jesus Christ. He did not give a final name to all he had received from the Lord until the end of his early letter to the Galatians. In Galatians 6:15, he called it a *new creation*. When the word *faith* is called a new creation, it is referring to it as a contrast to the works of the Law.

THE ROLE OF FAITH DEFINED TO THE GALATIANS

Earlier in Paul's letter, the faith of Abraham was used as an object lesson of divine revelation. Galatians 3:6 states that Abraham believed God before the Law was ever given, and it was credited to him as righteousness. The Apostle moved from that new insight to say that scripture was indicating that God would justify Gentiles (like the Galatians) by faith, and not by their keeping the Law. In Galatians 6:25, he said something that caught Martin Luther's mind and led to the Reformation. This "new creation" blends all believers into one mind and one heart. To understand this passage, we must define the word *faith*. The Greek dictionary defines the word as a composite of two similar words (a) *pistis* and (b) *pathos*. The first word implies *belief*, the second implies *feelings*. When the words are combined, the Greek word *pisteuos* is created and used for the word faith. The aspect of belief in the definition relates to the mind or cognition. The addition of the word *pathos* means *feelings* or in the heart domain.

In reading this we are reminded of the first promises of the New Covenant: "I will put **my law** (of righteousness) in their **minds** and I will write it in their **hearts**." Combined, the words stand for **faith**. The words *new creation* are referring to new beings being created from their faith in Christ, whether Jew or Gentile. A problem exists, according to Ephesians 2:8, "For it is by grace you have been saved, through faith, and this not from yourselves, it is the gift of God." When we are willing, God even gives faith. That surely applies to the New Covenant of grace. The word *grace* is *charis* (gift) in Greek, as we have mentioned before, in defining the word *eucharist*. Those believers, on the

FIGURE 8.1 *Martin Luther statue in Worms, Germany*
Photo courtesy of the author

FIGURE 8.2 *The gate in the wall at Worms, Germany where Luther escaped from his trial at the Diet of Worms*
Photo courtesy of the author

Day of Pentecost, were all given gifts from God to the Son:

> Now that **this faith has come**, we are no longer under a guardian. So in Christ Jesus **you are all children of God through faith**, for all of you who were baptized into Christ have clothed yourselves with Christ. There is neither Jew nor Gentile, neither slave nor free, nor is there male and female, for you are all one in Christ Jesus. If you belong to Christ, then you are Abraham's seed, and heirs according to the promise. (Galatians 3:25-29 NIV, Emphasis mine)

The Apostle introduced another insight regarding faith in Galatians 5:5. He warned those that were being oppressed by legalistic Jews to consider the fact that if one chose to be justified before God through the Law, they would have to keep all of it and not just circumcision. He drove home the main aspect of our faith when he wrote:

> You who are trying to be justified by the law have been alienated from Christ; **you have fallen away from grace**. For through the Spirit we eagerly await by faith the righteousness for which we hope. For in Christ Jesus neither circumcision nor uncircumcised has any value. The only thing that counts is faith expressing itself through love. (Galatians 5:4-6 NIV, Emphasis mine)

He introduced another reminder to them concerning faith when he used the term "new creation." The freedom from the Law did not mean they were free to live according to the desires of the old self. In Galatians 5:16, he made reference to them having a choice as to whether they wanted to live under the control of the Holy Spirit or their old sin nature. He began writing about issues covered under the New Covenant when he said that the sin nature desires that which is contrary to the Spirit. After he had given illustrations from the old nature, he contrasted them with the fruit of the Spirit. He then gave the result of God's last promise in the New Covenant. After that he would say:

> Those who belong to Christ Jesus have crucified the flesh with its passions and desires. Since we live by the Spirit, let us keep in step with the Spirit. Let us not become conceited, provoking and envying each other. (Galatians 5:24-26 NIV)

A NEW LAW OF RIGHTEOUSNESS DEFINED
FOR THE ROMANS

Paul identified himself to the Roman believers as an apostle set apart for the gospel of God. He longed to see them, so he could impart some spiritual gift to them from the Holy Spirit to make their faith even stronger.

He began by teaching the reaction of God to sin. The focus turned to the Law again as intended to clarify what is unrighteous. The Law was not intended to be a means to remove sin. Jesus had created a way that would remove sin or unrighteousness through faith. When he stated the way had already been described by some of the prophets, he was undoubtedly referring to Isaiah, Jeremiah and Ezekiel and their reference to the New Covenant. God graciously willed to remove unrighteousness through faith in His Son Jesus Christ. Paul gave an illustration:

But now apart from the law the righteousness of God has been made known, to which the Law and the Prophets testify. **This righteousness is given through faith in Jesus Christ to all who believe.** There is no difference between Jew and Gentile, for all have sinned and fall short of the glory of God, and all are justified freely by his grace through the redemption that came by Christ Jesus. (Romans 3:21-24 NIV, Emphasis mine)

In the New Covenant, God was promising to remove sin that had been made *visible* through the Law. It would be done graciously by God through a redemption that came by the Lord Jesus Christ through faith in His shed blood.

God presented Christ as a sacrifice of atonement, through the shedding of his blood—**to be received by faith**. He did this to demonstrate his righteousness, because in his forbearance he had left the sins committed beforehand unpunished—he did it to demonstrate his righteousness at the present time, so as to be just and the one who justifies those who have faith in Jesus. (Romans 3:25-26 NIV, Emphasis mine)

God revealed that through faith a man could be justified apart from the Law, as a result of God's promises in the New

Covenant. It could apply to making the righteousness accredited to Abraham become part of our new minds and hearts. God had a plan whereby He would declare both Jews and Gentiles justified through faith. This same truth was explained to Daniel, as the answer to his prayer for forgiveness recorded earlier (see Daniel 9:22).

> It was not through the law that Abraham and his offspring received the promise that he would be heir of the world, but through the righteousness that comes by faith. For if those who depend on the law are heirs, faith means nothing and the promise is worthless, because the law brings wrath. And **where there is no law there is no transgression**. Therefore, the promise comes by faith, so that it may be by grace and may be guaranteed to all Abraham's offspring—not only to those who are of the law but also to those who have the faith of Abraham. He is the father of us all. (Romans 4:13-16 NIV, Emphasis mine)

Chapter Eight of Romans stands out in Scripture as one of the most gracious and forgiving chapters in the Bible for those who are *in Christ*. Paul supported that with a personal testimony: "The Law of the Spirit of life set me free from the law of sin and death." Actually, the words he was using came out of his next revelation to be discussed in the following chapter.

It is worthwhile to list the insights given to Paul and to those of us who know the grace of God related to our faith in Christ. These verses from the eighth chapter of Romans convey so much of the Apostle's awakening and ours through him:

Therefore there is now no condemnation for those who are in Christ Jesus. (Romans 8:1 NASB)

For the mind set on the flesh is death, but the mind set on the Spirit is life and peace. (Romans 8:6 NASB)

But if anyone does not have the Spirit of Christ, he does not belong to Him. (Romans 8:9 NASB)

But if the Spirit of Him who raised Jesus from the dead dwells in you, He who raised Christ Jesus from the dead will also give life to your mortal bodies through His Spirit who dwells in you. (Romans 8:11 NASB)

For all who are being led by the Spirit of God, these **are sons of God**. (Romans 8:14 NASB, Emphasis mine)

The Spirit Himself testifies with our spirit that we **are children of God**, and if children, heirs also, heirs of

God and **fellow heirs with Christ**, if indeed we suffer with Him so that we may also be glorified with Him. (Romans 8:16-17 NASB, Emphasis mine)

The creation itself also will be set free from its slavery to corruption into the freedom of the glory of the **children of God**. (Romans 8:21 NASB, Emphasis mine)

For those whom He foreknew, He also predestined to become conformed to the image of His Son, so that He would be the firstborn among many brethren. (Romans 8:29 NASB)

If God is for us, who is against us? (Romans 8:31 NASB)

Who will separate us from the love of Christ? Will tribulation, or distress, or persecution, or famine, or nakedness, or peril, or sword? (Romans 8:35 NASB)

For I am convinced that neither death, nor life, nor angels, nor principalities, nor things present, nor things to come, nor powers, nor height, nor depth, nor any other created thing, will be able to separate us from the love of God, which is in Christ Jesus our Lord. (Romans 8:38-39 NASB)

The eighth chapter of Romans rates as one of the most revealing of all his writings. The Apostle's final advice to the Romans was to accept the Jews as Christ had accepted Gentiles, in order to bring praise to God. It was harder for the Jews in the city to accept the idea of being one with Gentiles. He closed with what he had been given about God's plans for Israel. He wrote that Christ had died for the Jews on behalf of God's truth, so that the promises made to the patriarchs might be confirmed, and that the Gentiles might glorify God for his mercy. We are all one in Christ. Paul saw that Isaiah had been given a similar inspiration of the future when he quoted from the prophet:

> "The Root of Jesse will spring up, one who will arise to rule over the nations; in him the Gentiles will hope." May the God of hope fill you with all joy and peace as you trust in him, so that you may overflow with hope by the power of the Holy Spirit. (Romans 15:12-13 NIV)

Paul's advice was based on what he had been taught and what he knew from the prophets.

The Cup Defined at Corinth

The letters he wrote to the Corinthian church reveal more
than he ever learned from his teacher Gemaliel as a Pharisee.
Corinth was an area in which Rome rewarded former soldiers, government workers and a few wealthy families with
property as rewards for past loyalties. The city was situated
in Achaia, a section of land that lay off the western coast of
Greece, connecting the Greek mainland and two seas. It was
the most ideally situated city for commerce and sea trade. The
city was stretched out along a wide stone pavement leading
up to a large Citadel with a Temple of Aphrodite at the top.
Sin was rampant in the evenings as prostitutes came down to
the city from the Temple of Aphrodite. It was into that envi-
ronment Paul and Silas entered on the third missionary trip.

The First Corinthian Letter Written
from Ephesus in 55ad

After praising the people for their reception of the grace of
God by faith, he began to appeal to them to grow up in their
knowledge of righteousness. He pointed out how distracting it
was to always be comparing him with Peter, Apollos or some
other teacher on the basis of their oratory. He urged them to
stop worshipping human wisdom and philosophies and to
seek the wisdom of God that only the Holy Spirit could reveal.
He asked them to abandon their temptations into sexual

immorality, so prevalent all around them. He wanted them to seek the wisdom of God over the wisdom of the world. He then turned their attention to some of the basics he had taught them on his first visit. He brought up the subject of the Last Supper and how they were abusing the truth he had taught them. He asked them to remember what he had taught them about **the Cup and the Covenant**:

> For I received from the Lord what I also passed on to you: The Lord Jesus, on the night he was betrayed, took bread, and when he had given thanks, he broke it and said, "This is my body, which is for you; do this in remembrance of me." In the same way, after supper he took the cup, saying, "This cup is the new covenant in my blood; do this, whenever you drink it, in remembrance of me. For whenever you eat this bread and drink this cup, you proclaim the Lord's death until he comes." (1 Corinthians 11:23-26 NIV)

Using that memory, he reminded them of his previous teaching: "You cannot drink the cup of the Lord and the cup of demons too." He knew the lifestyle of Corinth was a constant temptation. He gave them the wisdom he had been given:

No temptation has overtaken you except what is common to mankind. And God is faithful; he will not let you be tempted beyond what you can bear. But when you are tempted, he will also provide a way out so that you can endure it. (1 Corinthians 10:13 NIV)

That was the grace of God he had been taught.

Toward the end of his first letter, he opened their eyes to the future. In Chapter 15, he mentioned there was something he had been given to pass on to them regarding the resurrection of Christ and their own resurrection one day:

For what I received I passed on to you as of first importance: that Christ died for our sins according to the Scriptures, that he was buried, that he was raised on the third day according to the Scriptures, and that he appeared to Cephas, and then to the Twelve. After that, he appeared to more than five hundred of the brothers and sisters at the same time, most of whom are still living, though some have fallen asleep. Then he appeared to James, then to all the apostles, and last of all he appeared to me also, as to one abnormally born. (1 Corinthians 15:3-8 NIV)

Paul built on that knowledge by adding that Jesus was the first fruits of our own resurrection one day. He added some more information about our own resurrected bodies. Our resurrected bodies will be imperishable and spiritual like the resurrected Jesus. He used a comparison and contrast for a final example:

> The first man was of the dust of the earth; the second man is of heaven. As was the earthly man, so are those who are of the earth; and as is the heavenly man, so also are those who are of heaven And just as we have borne the image of the earthly man, so shall we bear the image of the heavenly man. (1 Corinthians 15:47-49 NIV)

God is working on His New Creation, maturing the new man.

THE SECOND LETTER TO THE CORINTHIAN CHURCH

Paul had planned earlier to visit them on his way back to Jerusalem with a charitable gift for those being persecuted by the Jews. We all benefitted from that change in plans, since we have the material he planned to teach them.

The grace of God is still at work when we recall the divine revelations given to Paul and read them for ourselves. God has used him to instruct us. The best is yet to come. How gracious of God to reveal to Paul that Gentiles were to be shown mercy along with Israel! The change in Paul should be in all of us who have been born again. The change is the love of God, and His Son is in our hearts and minds. The truths Paul put in 2 Corinthians are beyond comparison. His words, written under the Holy Spirit's enlightenment, have been a "fragrance of life and aroma of Christ to us as well." (see 2 Corinthians 2:16).

Thank you Lord and may it continue to be so!

GUIDED DISCOVERY

Note: Read Genesis 12:1-3 and 15:1-6 before answering.

1. How was the whole world blessed through Abraham? What was God's reward for his obedience?

2. What was the first divine revelation given to Paul that he called a new creation? How would this revelation apply to Gentiles?

3. Read Galatians 3:6-14. What did Paul write about a new creation called *faith*, that influenced Luther to lead the Protestant Reformation?

4. Explain in your own words, from reading this chapter, how faith in Christ leads to the fulfilling of the first two promises of the New Covenant.

5. In contrast to obedience, how does faith in Christ result in a greater reward than trying to be justified by keeping the Law?

6. How did Paul demonstrate that we are all children of Abraham—both Jew or Gentile—through faith in Christ?

7. How did faith in Christ fulfill the last two promises of the New Covenant?

8. How did the Apostle Paul use the Cup of the Last Supper to institute the practice of Communion, or the Eucharist, in churches today? What did he mean by the statement, "You cannot drink the cup of the Lord and the cup of demons too?"

CHAPTER NINE

Another Divine Revelation

E vidence that Paul had been given new information about the future of Israel, the Gentiles and something called a "new creation" can be seen in what he wrote in a second letter to Corinth. It was about two years after the first letter. He had been on three missionary journeys. The words "new creations" apply as a major aspect of the new divine revelation to Paul. The remainder would gradually come into focus by the time of the Roman letter. One cannot help but see the progression of truth.

He wrote the second Corinthian letter to explain the change in his plans to visit them again. In the letter he shared the persecutions he had faced, and the strengthening of his faith as he saw God's protection in each situation. He had wanted to share what God was doing in his life and in the world, so they could benefit from hearing and learning about the grace of God. It was not until the third chapter of 2 Corinthians that he was able to communicate his new excitement. He was not boasting about himself, but the renewed faith that God had given him.

THE REVELATION OF RESTORED RIGHTEOUSNESS

When he could hold back no longer, he began to share what God had revealed to him. **It was the connection between the New Covenant and a new creation God was forming through faith in Christ**. It thrilled him that he had been made a part of it. How could this have been so overlooked?

> Such confidence we have through Christ before God. Not that we are competent in ourselves to claim anything for ourselves, but our competence comes from God. **He has made us competent as ministers of a new covenant**—not of the letter but of the Spirit; for the letter kills, but the Spirit gives life. (2 Corinthians 3:4-6 NIV, Emphasis mine)

In verse nine, he shared the contrast between the law of righteousness (that leads to condemnation and death) with the goal of the New Covenant (which was designed to impute righteousness into believers). What thrilled him was that God was making Silas, Timothy and himself *competent ministers* of that new work. He noted that if people benefitted from keeping the Law, how much more they would receive from **being transformed into the likeness of Christ** with ever increasing glory (see 2 Corinthians 3:18). He revealed to us the blessed hope we have in our future.

He began to share with them his insights as to the meaning of such a relationship with God. He now knew that the One who raised the Lord from the dead would also raise him and his loved ones into the likeness of Jesus. He started Chapter Five of his second letter with thoughts about the changes that would take place in our own existences. His new zeal caused him to worry, lest they think he was overconfident. A brief flashback to the promises of God in the New Covenant—to restore righteousness in believers' hearts and minds, and to cleanse them from sin forever through the blood of Christ—helps us to understand his joy.

How comforting are his words to all believers who are outwardly suffering, aging and wasting away in any form of life, and to know that inwardly we are growing—belonging to a *new creation* called *the Body of Christ*. Evidently, God had revealed to him certain aspects of our intermediate bodies in heaven (while waiting for new bodies), since he wrote about this mystery revealed to him. He began to use personal pronouns like "we" and "ours" in his writing. He wrote:

For we know that if the earthly tent we live in is destroyed, we have a building from God, an eternal house in heaven, not built by human hands. Meanwhile we groan, longing to be clothed instead with our heavenly dwelling, because when we are clothed, we will not be found naked. For while we are in this tent, we groan and are burdened, because we do not wish to be unclothed but to be clothed instead with our heavenly dwelling, so that what is mortal may be swallowed up by life. Now the one who has fashioned us for this very purpose is God, who has given us the Spirit as a deposit, guaranteeing what is to come. (2 Corinthians 5:1-5 NIV)

A REVELATION OF RECONCILIATION WITH GOD

The more Paul contemplated being reborn into the image of Christ, the more he wanted to live like Him. He was compelled more to love and give of himself to others. In 2 Corinthians 5:17, he shared the discovery of his life: he was a new creation. If you are a believer, these words may resonate in your memories as you have matured:

Therefore, if anyone is in Christ, the **new creation** has come: The old has gone, the new is here! All this is from God, who **reconciled us to himself** through Christ and gave us the ministry of reconciliation: that God was reconciling the world to himself in Christ, not counting people's sins against them. And he has committed to us the message of reconciliation. We are therefore Christ's ambassadors, as though God were making his appeal through us. We implore you on Christ's behalf: **Be reconciled to God**. God made him who had no sin to be sin for us, so that in him we might become the righteousness of God. (2 Corinthians 5:17-21 NIV, Emphasis mine)

FINAL REVELATION OF THE MYSTERY

In his Ephesian letter, written from his first imprisonment in Rome around 62 AD, a new insight was expressed in his opening words: God had predestined us to be adopted as His sons through Jesus Christ. He made a reference to the New Covenant again when he wrote that we have been redeemed through Christ's shed blood, and received the forgiveness of sins according to the riches of God's grace. In Ephesians 1:9, he made reference to another mystery of God's will, that He will not put into effect until the end times. At that time, all things on heaven and on earth will be under one head, namely, Jesus Christ. He did not say how, but it was revealed to him by God's grace. He was referring to our inheritance in heaven one day:

Surely you have heard about the administration of God's grace that was given to me for you, that is, the mystery made known to me by revelation, as I have already written briefly. In reading this, then, you will be able to understand my insight into the mystery of Christ, which was not made known to people in other generations as it has now been revealed by the Spirit to God's holy apostles and prophets. **This mystery is that through the gospel the Gentiles are heirs together with Israel, members together of one body, and sharers together in the promise in Christ Jesus.** (Ephesians 3:2-6 NIV, Emphasis mine)

The statement *making Israel a co-heir with Gentiles* would have been intolerable without some further explanation. To make Gentiles co-heirs with Israel would have been blasphemy about God's purpose promised to the Jews. The mystery still is a puzzle to many who have not studied the word of God cover to cover and discovered the true meaning of the mystery. Reading the next section helps to understand his hope:

I became a servant of this gospel by the gift of God's grace given me through the working of his power. Although I am less than the least of all the Lord's people, this grace was given me: to preach to the Gentiles the boundless riches of Christ, and to make plain to everyone the administration of this mystery, which for ages past was kept hidden in God, who created all things. His intent was that **now, through the church,** the manifold wisdom of God should be made known to the rulers and authorities in the heavenly realms, according to his eternal purpose that he accomplished in Christ Jesus our Lord. In him and through faith in him we may approach God with freedom and confidence. (Ephesians 3:7-12 NIV, Emphasis mine)

The key to the mystery is found in the correct interpretation of the word *church*. The confusion still exists when we do not differentiate between the various interpretations of the word. To some, *church* refers to the first covenant given to Abraham. To others, it may mean the Catholic Church. To some, it may mean a building or some local sectarian organization. To grasp the meaning, Paul attached to the word "is to return" to the meaning Jesus gave to it, when He used it for the first time in Matthew 16:18.

Jesus began to introduce it early with Nicodemus in John 3:5 as a new spiritual birth. He added the familiar John 3:16 verse before He was finished. The prophets had referred to it as a *new creation* (see Isaiah 42:6-9). He had explained the means by which one enters into that new creation, or The Church, previously to Gentiles in Ephesians 2:11-22. It is what he meant in 2 Corinthians 5:17: "If anyone is in Christ, he is a new creation." Paul was explaining the mystery revealed to him was that by becoming a member of the Body of Christ, through faith and the indwelling of the Holy Spirit, the door was open to Israelites as well as to Gentiles. It is true that God was creating a new entity to exist along with Jews, Gentiles, called **the new body of Christ**. It is also true that nowhere does Paul ever teach that the church by any definition does away with the nationality of Israel and the promises made to them as a nation. To support that, one only needs to read his views expressed in Romans Chapters 9-11.

It may be wise to review the various distinctions of the word *church* again. No one has ever written the distinctions with more clarity than Lewis Sperry Chafer in his Systematic Theology, Vol. IV, p.34-35. He offered this explanation:

The one who cannot recognize that the **Church** is a new, heavenly purpose of God, absolutely dissociated from both Jew and Gentile (Galatians 3:28; Colossians 3:11), but sees the Church only as an ever increasing company of redeemed people gathered alike from all ages of human history, would do well to ponder the following questions: Why the "mysteries" of the New

Testament, including the Body of Christ? Why the New Creation, comprising as it does, all those who by the Spirit are joined to the Lord and are forever in Christ? How could there be a Church, constructed as she is, until the death of Christ, the resurrection of Christ, the ascension of Christ, and the Day of Pentecost? How could the Church (as it exists), be any part of Israel in this or any other age? (Emphasis mine)

The original Greek word, *ekklesias* for *church* is like the word for a car. To appreciate it you must know more about it. When was it made and by whom? For what purpose was it designed, and who is or was to be the principle owner? The church Paul was referring to was in the process of being built and designed by, and for, Jesus. It had not existed before, since He was **going to build it**. It would be built for people that were being created, and for people who were to form a body for Him and the Holy Spirit to indwell on Earth. It was a new creation referred to by the prophets (see Isaiah, Jeremiah and Ezekiel).

It would be created from believers in Christ's atonement for their sins, which meant that it would be necessary for Christ to give His life for them. Like others, it would be called out and predestined by the grace of God. It would be entered by Jews and Gentiles who would surrender their human identities, in order to be born again into the Body of Christ and family of God. It would be eternally spiritual and one that the "gates of hell" would not be able to destroy (see Matthew 16:18). With that background, it should never be miscast as created by human hands or minds. All that background makes it *organic* and not an *organized* church or building. That is the mystery Church Paul was describing in 2 Corinthians 5:17 and his other Epistles. **Lives would be made righteous by the promises of God in the New Covenant**. "I will put my law of righteousness in their hearts and minds."

During his first imprisonment in Rome around 62 AD, Paul wrote these words to the Colossians about the mystery of the Church for which he was rejoicing:

Now I rejoice in what I am suffering for you, and I fill up in my flesh what is still lacking in regard to Christ's afflictions, for the sake of his body, which is the church. I have become its servant by the commission God gave me to present to you the word of God in its fullness— the mystery that has been kept hidden for ages and generations, but is now disclosed to the Lord's people. To them God has chosen **to make known among the Gentiles the glorious riches of this mystery, which is Christ in you, the hope of glory**. He is the one we proclaim, admonishing and teaching everyone with all wisdom, so that we may present everyone fully mature in Christ. To this end I strenuously contend with all the energy Christ so powerfully works in me. (Colossians 1:24-29 NIV, Emphasis mine)

He asked them to pray for him that the door would be open for the message he had been given to deliver.

He had a very close relationship with Apollos at Corinth and Ephesus. He passed on to him what God had revealed to him about uniting their people into a new body of believers called the Church. He would have shared the connection that the New Covenant had with the forming of that New Creation. In the early years it was believed by some that Paul wrote the book of Hebrews before he died. Many of us, Martin Luther included, believe that Apollos had written it. Reason supports such a view as the author wrote that "This salvation was first announced by the Lord, and was **confirmed to us by those who heard Him**." (see Hebrews 2:3). Paul said that what he wrote came from the Lord Himself (see Galatians 1:11-12). Regardless, both Paul and Apollos had the same love for their Hebrew brothers. They also shared this eulogy for Jesus:

For both he that sanctifieth and they who are sanctified are all of one: for which cause he is not ashamed to call them brethren, Saying, I will declare thy name unto my brethren, in the midst of the church (ekklesias) will I sing praise unto thee. And again, I will put my trust in him. And again, Behold I and the children which God hath given me. Forasmuch then as the children are partakers of flesh and blood, he also himself likewise took part of the same; that through death he might destroy him that had the power of death, that is, the devil; And deliver them who through fear of death were all their lifetime subject to bondage. For verily he took not on him the nature of angels; but he took on him the seed of Abraham. Wherefore in all things it behoved him to be made like unto his brethren, that he might be a merciful and faithful high priest in things pertaining to God, to make reconciliation for the sins of the people. For in that he himself hath suffered being tempted, he is able to succour them that are tempted. (Hebrews 2:11-18 KJV, Clarification mine)

Apollos had been trained by Philo in Alexandria in Old Testament doctrine. We are blessed to read that it was Aquila and his wife Priscilla who took Apollos aside and explained the role of the Holy Spirit in the believer's life. Hebrews was written in 67AD while Paul was in prison (see Acts 18:24-26, 28).

The first contribution that Hebrews made was in explaining the role that Jesus played as our High Priest: making the propitiation atonement of the New Covenant a necessity to enter into the Body of Christ (see 1 John 2:2; Romans 3:25-26; Hebrews 10:1-10). He wrote like Paul, who may have told him:

> The law is only a shadow of the good things that are coming—not the realities themselves. For this reason it can never, by the same sacrifices repeated endlessly year after year, make perfect those who draw near to worship. Otherwise, would they not have stopped being offered? For the worshipers would have been cleansed once for all, and would no longer have felt guilty for their sins. But those sacrifices are an annual reminder of sins. It is impossible for the blood of bulls and goats to take away sins. Therefore, when Christ came into the world, he said: "Sacrifice and offering you did not desire, but a body you prepared for me; with burnt offerings and sin offerings you were not pleased." Then he said, "Here I am, I have come to do your will." He sets aside the first to establish the second. And by that will, we have been made holy through the sacrifice of the body of Jesus Christ once for all. (Hebrews 10:1-6, 9-10 NIV)

The word *Church*, with a capital 'C,' did not refer to a building, organization or sect; but only to the Body of Christ. It was and is a New Creation of God in which both Jew and Gentiles have been invited to become children of God. In doing so, all barriers and separators are done away creating the unity that Jesus prayed for after the supper in John Chapter 17. Our heritage has been made possible by the fact He paid the price to redeem us, forever establishing the fact that we belong to Him. Praise God!

GUIDED DISCOVERY

Note: Begin by reading 2 Corinthians Chapter 5 as background to this chapter.

1. Paul wrote them about another divine revelation given to him. What was it that excited him so much?

2. What was the result of being reconciled to God under the New Covenant that added to his new joy? He explained it in 2 Corinthians 5:17.

3. In what would have been blasphemy in the past, Paul wrote a letter to the Church at Ephesus about how both Jews and Gentiles were being made co-heirs with Christ. How did he explain it?

4. How did Lewis Sperry Chafer explain this could not have happened if the Church was primarily an extension of Israel, rather than a new "Body of Christ?"

5. When Paul stated that we have been born again, he did not mean we lose our original souls or identities, but our human natures. What is changed?

6. How did the writer of Hebrews 2:11-18 explain the way Jesus could make and call believers in Him "brothers and sisters"?

7. Explain the difference between the expiation atonement of the old covenant and the propitiation atonement Jesus made in Romans 3:25-26 and Hebrews 10:1-10.

CHAPTER TEN

Knowledge that Leads to Understanding

"I, the LORD, have called you in righteousness; I will take hold of your hand. I will keep you and will make you to be a covenant for the people and a light for the Gentiles." (Isaiah 42:6 NIV)

The above passage revealed God's feelings toward Israel when He sent the New Covenant to Jeremiah. The prophecy was intended to be a comfort for the nation that was returning home after seventy years of captivity in Babylon. God in His love for them had prepared a gift for each member of the nation of Israel. It was a new nature in a new covenant of grace. In the past, He had given covenants to Moses that were addressed to them as a nation. Almost obscured in the first reading of Jeremiah was a change in the way this new contract was to apply. Under the old covenant, Israel's leaders applied it as a mandate for the people as a whole. The New Covenant was to be applied to individuals, whether Jew or Gentile, resulting in new creatures called the Body of Christ or His Church. The new nature would answer Daniel's prayer for God to forgive his people for their transgressions (see Daniel Chapter 9).

The new gift was not without warning, for Jeremiah was given a hint in the introduction to the prophecy:

> "For I know the plans I have for you," declares the LORD, "plans to prosper you and not to harm you, plans to give you hope and a future. Then you will call on me and come and pray to me, and I will listen to you. You will seek me and find me when you seek me with all your heart." (Jeremiah 29:11-13 NIV)

He was reminded that in the past, the sins of the fathers were passed on to their children. After the quote, God reminded His prophet of the changes coming when He followed up with a warning of the change to individual responsibility:

> "In those days people will no longer say, 'The parents have eaten sour grapes, and the children's teeth are set on edge.' Instead (now), everyone will die for his own

sin; whoever eats sour grapes—their own teeth will be set on edge. "This is the covenant **I will** make with the people of Israel after that time," declares the LORD. (Jeremiah 31:29-30, 33 NIV, Clarification and emphasis mine)

Changes were to take place in (a) the recipients from *fathers* to *individuals*, (b) from the nation to a family called the Children of God (or the body of Christ) and (c) Jesus would be the Head of the new body—the Church He was going to build that would include both Jews and Gentiles (see Matthew 16:18):

"**I will** put my law in their minds and write it on their hearts. **I will** be their God, and **they will be** my people. No longer will they teach their neighbor, or say to one another, 'Know the LORD,' because **they will all know me**, from the least of them to the greatest," declares the LORD. "**For I will forgive** their wickedness **and will remember their sins no more**." (Jeremiah. 31:33-34 NIV, Emphasis mine)

On the morning I had planned to write this chapter, I became aware of an alliteration of how the efforts of the Father, the Son and the Holy Spirit unite to create the New Covenant for the lives of individuals. The knowledge is a divine gift

when we see the unity of God moving toward His goal of reconciliation, "The Father **Wills**, the Son provides the **Way**, and
the Spirit **Works** to empower the fulfillment of the promises.
The insights are supported by Scripture, inspired by the Holy
Spirit. Many have accepted Jesus after He died, the rest are
still under the condemnation stemming from the sins of the
Fathers, compounded by their own.

These truths were supported and delivered later by those
who gave their lives to pass it on to others. In this chapter, we
see God taking full responsibility for fulfilling His *will*, with a
way provided by faith in Jesus, along with the *work* of the Holy
Spirit fulfilling the New Covenant. All that was required was
to accept the gift by faith in Jesus to provide the way.

THE FATHER'S WILL SEEN IN THE COVENANT OF GRACE

The use of the word *will* in describing God's new covenant
must never be interpreted as a last will or testament. God
was not dispensing any possessions. He was making promises about something He was going to create. He was promising to supply, in the future, an act of grace leading to eternal
life. To fulfill His promises in a new covenant of grace, He
willed to restore righteousness in our natures and to forgive
our sins by:

a. Sending His only begotten Son to die on a cross, as payment for our sin (John 3:16).

b. Sending His Holy Spirit to regenerate, create new natures in us (Acts 2:1-8).

c. Forgiving and being reconciled to believers as a result of an eternal atonement (1 John 2:2).

d. Honoring the Son's prayer, to indwell all who believe in Christ (John 17:22-23).

e. Making us His children in a new family (John 1:12).

See what great love the Father has lavished on us, that we should be called **children of God**! And that is what we are! The reason the world does not know us is that it did not know him." (1 John: 3:1 NIV, Emphasis mine)

The first two promises were to restore something we did not inherit, a righteous nature. The last two promises were to forgive sins and to forget them by accepting His plan or will. His plan was to restore the righteousness that Adam had lost. The plan called for His Son to assume the guilt and take it away:

He made known to us the mystery of his will according to his good pleasure, which he purposed in Christ, to be put into effect when the times reach their fulfillment—to bring unity to all things in heaven and on earth under Christ. In him we were also chosen, having been predestined according to the plan of him who works out everything in conformity with the purpose of his will, in order that we, who were the first to put our hope in Christ, might be for the praise of his glory. And you also were included in Christ when you heard the message of truth, the gospel of your salvation. When you believed, you were marked in him **with a seal, the promised Holy Spirit**. (Ephesians 1:9-13 NIV, Emphasis mine)

After the leaders and the nation rejected the gift and had Jesus crucified, God offered it to individuals, even Gentiles, who were willing to receive His Son as Savior. The first offer to an individual took place when Nicodemus, a Pharisee, approached Jesus at night. He was looking for signs of the coming of Messiah. Jesus chose to open the door of knowledge of God's will by saying "You must be born again." We know from Scripture that one of Israel's respected leaders, Nicodemus believed because he came to the cross to claim the body of Jesus.

THE SON PROVIDED THE WAY BY BECOMING AN OBJECT OF FAITH

The most difficult part for Jesus was to take all our sins upon His Holy body. His first cup of redemption was to suffer. He had five tasks to perform as a *way* for the fulfillment of the Father's plan. He had to:

a. **Become Our Redeemer.** In His role as our Savior, Jesus had to give His own life for us. Jesus answered, "**I am the way the truth and the life**. No one comes to the Father except through me." (John 14:6).

b. **Drain His Cup.** He had to suffer, provide the blood for an eternal atonement for our forgiveness and to mediate the New Covenant (1 John 2:2).

c. **Serve as Our High Priest.** He was resurrected as our high priest in order to take His blood into Heaven and place it on the Mercy Seat (Hebrews 9:12).

d. **Become the Head.** He gave birth to a Church called the Body of Christ. He established membership in that by faith in His death on the cross (Ephesians 2:8).

e. **Become our Blessed Hope** by coming with the Holy Spirit on Pentecost to live within us:

> He is before all things, and in him all things hold together. And he is the head of the body, **the Church**; he is the beginning and the firstborn from among the dead, so that in everything he might have the supremacy...the mystery that had been kept hidden for ages and generations, but is now disclosed to the Lord's people. To them God has chosen **to make known** among the Gentiles the glorious riches of this mystery, which is **Christ in you, the hope of glory**. (Colossians 1:17-18, 26-27 NIV, Emphasis mine)

THE WORKS OF THE HOLY SPIRIT'S POWER

The magnitude of the Holy Spirit's power in executing the will and ways of God extend from *hovering over the waters* in Genesis 1, to His role in generating the humanity of Christ in Mary. His work was to carry out God's will. His first contribution to the New Covenant was to empower all that was promised such as:

a. The generation of humanity in Jesus.

> The angel answered, "The Holy Spirit will come on you, and the power of the Most High will overshadow you. So the holy one to be born will be called the Son of God." (Luke 1:35 NIV)

b. The regeneration and resurrection of Christ from the grave.

> And if the Spirit of him that **raised** up Jesus from the dead dwell in you, he that **raised** up Christ from the dead shall also quicken your mortal bodies by his Spirit who lives in you. (Romans 8:11 NIV, Emphasis mine)

c. The regeneration of the disciples on the Day of Pentecost.

> All of them were filled with the Holy Spirit and began to speak in other tongues as the Spirit enabled them. (Acts 2:4 NIV)

d. Regenerate the divine nature into Jewish believers (Day of Pentecost).

e. Seal the promises of God within us (by remaining in all who believe).

> Now it is God who makes both us and you stand firm in Christ. He anointed us, **set his seal** of ownership on us, and put his Spirit in our hearts as a deposit, guaranteeing what is to come. (2 Corinthians 1:21-22 NIV, Emphasis mine)

THE TRANSITION TO INDIVIDUAL HEARTS AND MINDS

In Review

The first sign of a movement of God's grace from the nation to individuals was displayed in the dialogue between Jesus and Nicodemus. It was no accident that it was expressed to one of the pillars of Judaism, the Pharisee Nicodemus. Jesus spoke truth to him as an individual, not as a Jew or a Pharisee, but as a man seeking truth. He knew the man was asking about the future for Pharisees who believed in the resurrection after death. The Apostle John described the meeting:

Jesus Teaching Nicodemus

> Now there was a Pharisee, a man named Nicodemus who was a member of the Jewish ruling council. He came to Jesus at night and said, "Rabbi, we know that

you are a teacher who has come from God. For no one could perform the signs you are doing if God were not with him." Jesus replied, "Very truly I tell you, no one can see the kingdom of God unless they are born again." "How can someone be born when they are old?" Nicodemus asked. "Surely they cannot enter a second time into their mother's womb to be born!" Jesus answered, "Very truly I tell you, no one can enter the kingdom of God unless they are born of water and the Spirit. Flesh gives birth to flesh, but the Spirit gives birth to spirit. You should not be surprised at my saying, 'You must be born again.'" (John 3:1-7 NIV)

Knowing the man did not understand entirely, Jesus gave him a verse that has helped many of us to organize our faith in Christ:

For God so loved the world that he gave his one and only Son, that whoever believes in him shall not perish but have eternal life. For God did not send his Son into the world to condemn the world, but to save the world through him. Whoever believes in him is not condemned, but whoever does not believe stands condemned already because they have not believed in the name of God's one and only Son. (John 3:16-18 NIV)

Jesus Teaching a Woman in Samaria

The new message of salvation is open to individuals, even Samaritans:

"Sir," the woman said, "I can see that you are a prophet. Our ancestors worshiped on this mountain, but you Jews claim that the place where we must worship is in Jerusalem." "Woman," Jesus replied, "believe me, a time is coming when you will worship the Father neither on this mountain nor in Jerusalem. You Samaritans worship what you do not know; we worship what we do know, for salvation is from the Jews. Yet a time is coming and has now come when the true worshipers will worship the Father in the Spirit and in truth, for they are the kind of worshipers the Father seeks. God is spirit, and his worshipers must worship in the Spirit and in truth." The woman said, "I know that Messiah (called Christ) is coming. When he comes, he will explain everything to us." Then Jesus declared, "I, the one speaking to you—I am he." (John 4:19-26 NIV)

How can one not admire the "hutzpah" of Jesus, in presenting the truth as to the Father's will concerning how people are to worship Him? The result was that the woman and many of the Samaritans believed in Jesus because of her testimony (see John 4:39). The change to a focus on individuals can be seen in another truth. The word *church* was changing.

Before He left the upper room after the Last Supper, Jesus prayed a request to the Father that became the key to the door of understanding the divine nature. He asked that the new nature for individuals be created with same unity that existed in the divine nature:

> "My prayer is not for them alone. I pray also for those who will believe in me through their message, that all of them **may be one**, Father, just as you are in me and I am in you. **May they also be in us** so that the world may believe that you have sent me. I have given them the glory that you gave me, **that they may be one as we are one—I in them and you in me—so that they may be brought to complete unity**. Then the world will know that you sent me and have loved them even as you have loved me. **Father, I want those you have given me to be with me where I am, and to see my glory.**" (John 17:20-24 NIV, Emphasis mine)

Jesus provided a preview of our divine natures after we believe. We are indwelt by the Father, Son and Holy Spirit. The unity He prayed for lies within us, but becomes a reality only when we choose to live and walk in the Spirit. Paul taught us that if we choose to live in the flesh—the home of our old nature—we will experience conflict, for the two domains are at war within us.

The regeneration of our natures as a gift from God is something so new it is often called a new creation. It is not a reworking of the old nature, it is a new nature in the image of Christ, existing in the human body while on earth. The old will die with the body.

THE DIVINE PURPOSE WAS FOR CHILDREN OF GOD BE BORN OF THE SPIRIT

The manifestation of the New Covenant, according to the divine purpose, was to create, by regeneration, a new nature in all who are born again. All of which is accomplished by the gracious *will* of God, through faith in the *way* of Christ's death for our sins and the regenerative *works* of the Holy Spirit. The presence of the Divine Nature within us, according to the Word of God, seals the fact that we are children of God, heirs of God and joint-heirs with Christ through the adoption by the Holy Spirit. All of what follows is justified in God's covenant:

> For those who are led by the Spirit of God are the children of God. The Spirit you received does not make you slaves, so that you live in fear again; rather, the Spirit

you received brought about your adoption to sonship. And by him we cry, "*Abba*, Father." The Spirit himself testifies with our spirit that we are God's children. Now if we are children, then we are heirs—heirs of God and co-heirs with Christ, if indeed we share in his sufferings in order that we may also share in his glory. (Romans 8:14-17 NIV)

THE DIVINE PURPOSE FORGIVES SINS
AND REMEMBERS THEM NO MORE

What a gracious statement to make as the last set of promises. The Father did not have to add them for any other reason than to show us how much He loves those who belong to Him. It meant much to David, Peter and Paul. We know very few close friends that would be able to say that and mean it, if we had done something that hurt them in the past. He said that to show us the extent of His love.

Jesus gave another example of *agape,* or unconditional love, in the upper room when He was saying good-bye to His disciples. He knew the time had come to finish what the Father has sent Him to complete. John never forgot what He said:

My command is this: Love each other as I have loved you. Greater love has no one than this: to lay down one's life for one's friends. You are my friends if you do what I command. (John 15:12-14 NIV)

Years later, John gave us an application from the New Covenant:

This is how we know what love is: Jesus Christ laid down his **life** for us. And we ought to **lay down** our lives for our brothers and sisters. (1 John 3:16 NIV, Emphasis mine)

How unfortunate that so little is taught about the role of the New Covenant in Christian history. In it we are made aware of: (a) the great atonement, (b) a new body of individual believers called *The Church*, (c) made new creatures with righteous minds and hearts, (d) being recipients of total forgiveness, (e) becoming a co-heir with Christ and (f) the love and grace of God sending His own Son and Holy Spirit to recreate our natures. And, all of us who are in Christ and He in us will be resurrected to eternal life. How beneficial is that to all us?

The statement that, "without knowledge, there can be no understanding," stimulated the writing of this book, as I remembered my naivete when I first read the New Covenant passage in Jeremiah. I was thrilled to read all those promises, until I saw that it was promised to Israel. As I continued to read the Bible, my knowledge increased until I understood the value of the New Covenant, and how important it was to both Jews and Gentiles. When one understands the difference between atonement in the Old Testament and the atonement of Jesus, he or she comes to understand the difference between being credited with righteousness and being made righteous.

Our new nature exists in the image of Christ. We all need to ask ourselves, "Do I have someone in my life who has hurt me?" I have been asked to forgive them. In my new nature, there is power enough to do it. I know I should do it, for to will is within me to choose to forgive. The Holy Spirit has the power to remove a wrong from memory. Jesus did it on the cross (see Luke 23:24) and Stephen did it as he was being stoned (see Acts 7:60). Now we have the knowledge and now we understand: the nature we choose to live under will decide the answer.

GUIDED DISCOVERY

Note: God has not forgotten His people Israel. Jesus is still their Messiah. He also has brought light unto Gentiles. He has appealed to individuals, not just nations.

1. How did God answer Daniel's prayer with the New Covenant?

2. The New Covenant is an unconditional set of promises that begin with the words **I will**. That indicates that it began with the Father. Explain in your own words the involvement of the Son and the Spirit in carrying put His will.

3. Give evidence from the chapter of God's grace expressed in what He willed.

4. What is the main purpose of God's will, now that the mystery has been revealed? (see Ephesians 1:9).

5. What were some of the "ways" Jesus contributed to the New Covenant?

6. Explain how God chose to express His will by revealing the mystery of His Divine Riches to Gentiles.

7. Choose three of the five works of the Holy Spirit in executing the will of the Father, and explain why they are of the most importance to you.

8. Share what stood out to you from this chapter and explain why.

CHAPTER ELEVEN

Building a New Family

The foundation of the new Church was the New Covenant promises of God carried out in the lives of those who placed their faith in the blood of Christ. Unlike Abraham, they were not credited with righteousness, they were made righteous through a new birth. Jesus made that clear in John 3:3, when He said to Nicodemus: "No one can see the kingdom of God unless he is born again." When it became clear that the purpose of the New Covenant was to call out believers from the Jews and the Gentiles, a Church that God could make righteous through faith (in the death, resurrection, and atonement of Jesus), Christianity was born.

WHO WE WERE

Gentiles were aliens to the covenants of Israel when Christ came into humanity. The prophets Hosea and Isaiah were given insights into a grace of God: to unite two groups of people into a new family of men and women, who were not His people prior to a new covenant He had designed for Israel (only to have them reject it). Romans 9:23-26 reveals *who we were, who we are,* and *what we will be,* thanks to the New Covenant, if we receive it by faith in Jesus. No one explained who we Gentiles were better than the one selected to be our Apostle:

> And that he might make known the riches of his glory on the vessels of mercy, which he had afore prepared unto glory, Even us, whom he hath called, not of the Jews only, but also of the Gentiles? As he says also in Hosea, I will call them my people, which were not my people; and her beloved, which was not beloved. And it shall come to pass, that in the place where it was said unto them, Ye are not my people; there shall they be called the children of the living God. Isaiah also crieth concerning Israel, Though the number of the children of Israel be as the sand of the sea, a remnant shall be saved. (Romans 9:23-27 KJV)

Jesus called both Jew and Gentiles to be united by faith in Him. On the basis of that faith, we move from where we were to where we are, in Him and He in us, which becomes His Body in His Church in Matthew 16:18. The New Covenant was the doorway through which both groups enter as a new creation.

So Christ himself gave the apostles, the prophets, the evangelists, the pastors and teachers, to equip his people for works of service, so that the body of Christ may be built up until we all reach unity in the faith and in the knowledge of the Son of God and become mature, attaining to the whole measure of the fullness of Christ. (Ephesians 4:11-13 NIV)

To sustain His relationship with them, God sent His Holy Spirit to create righteous new natures in us and adopted us as His children with Christ as the Head. He had added another creation to His original cast of Jews and Gentiles. In 2 Corinthians 5:17, Paul called it a mystery that had been destined before time began.

A problem is raised in many churches when they view the church having begun with the covenant with Abraham. They view the church of today as a continuation of the church of Israel based on the promise to Abraham in Genesis 12:3: "all people on earth will be blessed through you." Those who disagree see that as a promise fulfilled in the lineage of Christ (see Matthew 1:2-16). The term *ekklesia* originally represented a gathering of Israelites in the Old Testament. As a religious group, it was replaced by the word *synagogue* (see Acts Chapter 9). The word *ekklesias* was used for a group of *called out ones* by Jesus as *my Church* in Matthew 16:18. It was not the same as the church of Israel, since Jesus said He was going to build His Church on the foundation of faith. If that is understood, the Church Christ was referring to was given birth on the Day of Pentecost (see Acts Chapter 2). All of these divisions in beliefs are the work of the enemy splitting God's truth. If nothing had changed, we all would still be under the Law and have no hope.

The time has come to examine who we are really are as believers in Christ today. We are not looking or waiting for a kingdom on this earth, nor are we capable of facing our maker without a new nature and a new heart. Here is where we are based on the great "Magna Carta" of all foundations called, The New Covenant. It should not surprise us that the enemy would attempt to erase all memory or teaching about it by keeping us under a standard no one but Jesus could uphold. Abraham was not under the Law; he only wanted to be obedient to God. For that reason, it was credited to him as righteousness. He had divine insight when he was tested, when he was asked to take his promised son Isaac—his only son by Sarah—to a mountaintop and offer him as a sacrifice. He knew burnt offerings were something pagans did to satisfy the wrath of their self-conceived gods, but he did as he was told and asked his servants to wait while he and Isaac went up the mountain. At that point, he revealed the first of three signs of faith. He said to the men, "Stay here with the boy's donkey while we go to worship and we will come back to you." The second sign of his faith was his answer to his son, who asked, "Father, we have the wood and the fire, but where is the lamb for the burnt offering?" Abraham answered, "God Himself will provide the lamb for the burnt offering my son." After they reached to top, we read that he tied his son Isaac and placed him in the stack of wood and picked up a knife to kill his son. At that point an angel called out from heaven saying, "Do not lay a hand on the boy for we know now you fear or stand in awe of God because you were willing to give up your son, your only true son." It was then that Abraham saw a ram caught by its horns in a thicket. He took the ram and sacrificed it instead of his son. He gave a new name to the place, *The Lord Provides*. Moses wrote and predicted, "On the Mountain of the Lord it will be provided." (Genesis Chapter 22). At the end of the chapter Moses wrote that God said to Abraham:

"I swear by myself, declares the LORD, that because you have done this and have not withheld your son, your only son, I will surely bless you and make your descendants as numerous as the stars in the sky and as the sand on the seashore. Your descendants will take possession of the cities of their enemies, and through your offspring all nations on earth will be blessed because you have obeyed me." (Genesis 22:16-18 NIV)

The power of that experience was what caused so many to believe that the Church actually started with Abraham. The last sentence was referring to Jesus being born to Mary in the lineage of Abraham, not the Church that Jesus said He was building on the foundation of faith under a New Covenant. Abraham was credited with righteousness for obeying God. That would have been the extent of our salvation, without the death of Christ and the indwelling of the Holy Spirit, if the church was only a continuation of Israel. If we were still under the Law, God would not have sent the prophecy of a new covenant to Jeremiah nor would He have sent His Son to die on a cross. The rest of this study will be directed toward the reason God sent a new covenant with an indwelling of His Spirit, on the day of Pentecost to make us new creatures in Christ. Our focus will not be on where we were, but on who we are now in the body of Christ and how we got there. Our genesis and new mandate may be Romans Chapter 8.

WHO WE ARE

We are, through faith in Christ, the beneficiaries and recipients of the love and grace of God expressed in a new covenant. To exclude that from our doctrine, our hope for the future, any forgiveness of sin, or Holy Spirit abiding in us, membership in God's family as a joint heir with Christ, or a new mind, or new heart, we would of all people be most miserable. That is the import of this study, supported by our representative, Paul, Apostle to Gentles:

> Therefore, there is now no condemnation for those who are in Christ Jesus, because through Christ Jesus the law of the Spirit who gives life has set you free from the law of sin and death. For what the law was powerless to do because it was weakened by the flesh, God did by sending his own Son in the likeness of sinful flesh to be a sin offering. And so he condemned sin in the flesh, in order that the righteous requirement of the law might be fully met in us, who do not live according to the flesh but according to the Spirit. (Romans 8:1-4 NIV)

Here is another benefit of the first two promises made to us in the New Covenant, applied to us:

> Those who live according to the flesh have their minds set on what the flesh desires; but those who live in accordance with the Spirit have their minds set on what the Spirit desires. The mind governed by the flesh is death, but the mind governed by the Spirit is life and peace. The mind governed by the flesh is hostile to God; it does not submit to God's law, nor can it do so. Those who are in the realm of the flesh cannot please God.

You, however, are not in the realm of the flesh but are in
the realm of the Spirit, if indeed the Spirit of God lives
in you. And if anyone does not have the Spirit of Christ,
they do not belong to Christ. (Romans 8:5-9 NIV)

We now know that there are many reasons why Christ had
to become human and Deity in one body. He had to die and
become the first-fruits of a resurrection that would make possible a church wherein both Jews and Gentiles could become
united into one body. The mystery that both Jews and Gentiles
could be born into a new body or family of believers was first
revealed to Peter, according to Luke in Acts Chapter 10.

With some misgivings, Peter obeyed God and responded
to a call from a Gentile named Cornelius, a Roman Centurion,
who believed in the Hebrew God. When Peter was asked to
enter the man's home to speak to his family and friends, he
was tested. He wanted the man to know that it was against
the law of the Jews to enter the house of a Gentile who was
considered *unclean*. He added, "God has shown me that we
are not to call any man impure." He then demonstrated the
kind of faith upon which Jesus said He was going to build
His Church. Peter went in and shared the gospel of Jesus with
Cornelius and his family and friends. He explained the reason Jesus had come to earth. He explained that everyone who
believes in Jesus receives forgiveness of sins through faith in

Him. As he was speaking, the Holy Spirit came upon all who heard the message; the same way he and the disciples had on the Day of Pentecost. The six circumcised believers that had accompanied Peter were shocked that the Holy Spirit had been poured out on Gentiles. Peter was given the honor of sharing the gospel with them.

In Acts 15:6, Peter stood before the first Church Council of Jerusalem to discuss whether Gentile believers should be circumcised. He shared his experience of seeing the coming of the Holy Spirit and His indwelling of uncircumcised Gentiles in the home of Cornelius. He and the six witnesses all saw the same signs given to verify their new natures. Peter asked, "Who was I that I should oppose God?" After Peter explained they had been baptized, the Church at Jerusalem praised God's grace and said, "So then, God has granted even the Gentiles repentance unto life." (see Acts 11:18).

That same message applies to all of us who have believed in Christ. It is by grace that all believers have a privileged position in the family of God. Some may not be aware of the "riches of divine grace" they have, if they have not read or understood the promises of the New Covenant. I have been amazed at the number of people I have asked, who told me they are Christians, through faith in Christ, but have had no teaching on the New Covenant. For that reason, what follows is a condensed set of riches, taught by Paul and the others, that have been inherited by all of us who have become a member of God's family, by faith in Jesus' death and atonement for our sins. This is Who We Are! Each gift will be followed by a comment and verses that support the gift:

Redemption

This is the primary gift that applies to all who believe. It is ours through the first two promises of the New Covenant, "I will put my laws (of righteousness) in their minds, and write them on their hearts." These verses supports the gift and the promises:

> This righteousness is given through faith in Jesus Christ to all who believe...for all have sinned and fall short of the glory of God, and are justified freely by his grace through the redemption that came by Jesus Christ. (Romans 3:22-24 NIV)

> In him we have redemption through his blood, the forgiveness of sins, in accordance with the riches of God's grace. (Ephesians 1:7 NIV)

Reconciliation

This gift is the result of being under the New Covenant that is mediated within us when we believe. It comes to us by faith in the merits in Jesus as supported in these verses:

Therefore, if anyone is in Christ, the new creation has come: The old has gone, the new is here! All this is from God, who reconciled us to himself through Christ and gave us the ministry of reconciliation: that God was reconciling the world to himself in Christ, not counting man's sins against them (the last promise). (2 Corinthians 5:16-19 NIV, Clarification mine)

Propitiation Atonement
Being treated as if I had never sinned, as seen in:

God presented him as a sacrifice of atonement, through faith in his blood…he did it to demonstrate his justice at the present time, so as to be just and the one who justifies those who have faith in Jesus. (Romans 3:25-26 NIV; cf. 1 John 2:2 NIV)

Made Children of God (Sons of God)
Being born again of the Holy Spirit, we enter the family of God:

See what great love the Father has lavished on us, that we should be called children of God! And that is **who we are**! (1 John 3:1 NIV, Emphasis mine)

Yet to all who did receive him, to those who believed in his name, he gave the right to become children of God. (John 1:12 NIV)

Gifts of God to Jesus

At least seven times in his high priestly prayer in John 17, Jesus used the term, "all those you have given to me." The following are excerpts:

For you granted him authority over all people that he might give eternal life to all those you have given him. (John 17:2 NIV)

I pray for them. I am not praying for the world, but for those you have given me, for they are yours. (John 17:9 NIV)

"Father, I want those you have given me to be with me where I am, and to see my glory, the glory you have given me because you loved me before the creation of the world." (John 17:24 NIV)

Objects of God's Love

The all time favorite has been:

For God so loved the world that he gave his one and only Son, that whoever believes in him shall not perish but have eternal life. (John 3:16 NIV)

But God demonstrates his own love for us in this: While we were still sinners, Christ died for us. (Romans 5:8 NIV; cf. 1 Thessalonians 1:4)

Unity in Our New Nature
The enemy may have divided the churches' doctrines, but the Holy Spirit has maintained the unity we have inwardly with God:

Father, just as you are in me and I am in you. May they also be in us so that the world may believe that you have sent me...so that they may be brought to complete unity. Then the world will know that you sent me and have loved them even as you have loved me. (John 17:21, 23 NIV)

Eternal Security
The eighth chapter of Romans begins with the truth that we are not under condemnation and ends with he assurance that nothing can separate us from the love of God:

Therefore, there is now no condemnation for those who
are in Christ Jesus. (Romans 8:1 NIV)

Neither height nor depth, nor any thing else in all creation that can separate us from the love of God that is
in Christ Jesus our Lord. (Romans 8:39 NIV)

CONCLUSIONS

It has been painful to write and read about how oblivious
many are about the promises of the New Covenant. That was
not the case during the first century after the death of Christ.
The Apostles were all competent ministers of the New Covenant. The enemy set up road blocks to the truth in a variety
of ways after Constantine made Christianity an enforced national religion.

This study began with a prayer that the New Covenant
might be brought back into our consciousness. The Apostle
Paul was selected and prepared to take the promise of the
New Covenant to Gentiles. He is the logical one to restore our
memories of God's love in restoring both Jews and Gentiles
to Himself as new born creations and children born again
into the image of Christ. His letter to the Galatians helped influence believers to see the truth about justification through
faith in Christ. In his letters to the Ephesians, Romans and the
Corinthians, he shared the revelations given to him about the

New Covenant and the uniqueness of the body of Christ in His Church. The list that follows is a must read if one is interested in what God has made possible for both Jews and Gentiles that want to be with Him in Eternity.

Read Paul's letter to the Ephesians, in which he outlines and defines all that God has accomplished in sending His Son to die for our sins and sent His Holy Spirit to make us into new creations, whom He calls His children. Read 2 Corinthians 5:16-21 to learn how God revealed to him the pathway to righteousness and a being born again. Read as a climax what he wrote about a mystery revealed to him, in Colossians 1:26-27, about being "in Christ and having Christ in us." All of which is promised in the New Covenant.

It should not surprise us that the enemy would do all in his power to remove the knowledge of God's love and grace from so many in these latter days. The truth is being made known again, to all who are willing to receive it. Christ came into humanity at a midpoint in human history to restore the righteousness that was lost with Adam's sin. How gracious of Him to reveal His final offer of grace one more time for all who seek Him. One of the better summaries of that grace was written to be read in Ephesians 3:5-12. It needs to be shared once again by those who know Him.

GUIDED DISCOVERY

Note: Apply each of the two subtitles to yourself from this chapter.

1. Who were you before you became a recipient the New Covenant?

2. Who are you now, based upon your understanding of the Covenant? Explain as fully as possible.

3. A list of riches appears in this chapter. Which one is most cherished by you as a gift from God?

4. What pleased you most from Christ's response to God for giving you to Him? Explain.

5. The unity we have within us will never be taken away. What did the enemy do to splinter us outwardly into so many diverse groups?

6. How has God overcome all the outward diversity once we are in heaven?

7. In what we know about the history of His Church, where do we see the Grace of God most clearly?

CHAPTER TWELVE

The Cornerstone
of the
New Covenant

As you come to him, the living Stone—rejected by humans but chosen by God and precious to him—you also, like living stones, are being built into a spiritual house to be a holy priesthood, offering spiritual sacrifices acceptable to God through Jesus Christ. For in Scripture it says: "See, I lay a stone in Zion a chosen and **precious cornerstone**, and the one who trusts in him will never be put to shame." Now to you who believe, this stone is precious. But to those who do not believe, "The stone the builders rejected has become **the cornerstone**," and, "A stone that causes people to stumble and a rock that makes them fall." They stumble because they disobey the message—which is also what they were destined for. (1 Peter 2:4-8 NIV, Emphasis mine)

Miss A. Wetherell Johnson, former missionary to China and founder of Bible Study Fellowship, successfully taught the Bible with this advice: "Read the Bible passage in context and ask yourself three questions when you finish a section: 'What did it say?' 'What did it mean?' and 'How does it apply to me?'" We have tried to follow that pattern in this study.

WHAT DID IT SAY?

We started reading the history and early uses of the words for church in the Old Testament. We found that the word church was derived from the Koine Greek word *ekklesias*. The word was applied to gatherings of people called to organize themselves for a purpose. The earliest was a group of people called Israel, whom God had called out of slavery in Egypt. Their patriarch was a man called Abraham, to whom God had made a covenant to provide him with a family that would become a nation in time. In that same covenant, God promised to give him a son, born to his wife Sarah, that would be a progenitor, or seed, from which the nation would develop and be known as the people of God. In that sense, Israel or Judaism became a people of God. God had their Messiah born in the lineage of Abraham, from which the world has been blessed.

God sent Jesus with a New Covenant of grace, in which the national leaders refused to accept. All of those things are a part of their history as recorded in God's Word. In 70AD, God removed them from the land and allowed the Temple to be destroyed. That is what the Scriptures say to us. Does that mean that God has forsaken Israel? The apostle Paul denies that Israel has been deserted by God. He claimed that they will be given another opportunity in which they will receive their Messiah immediately:

> I do not want you to be ignorant of this mystery, brothers and sisters, so that you may not be conceited: Israel has experienced a hardening in part until the full number of the Gentiles has come in, and in this way all Israel will be saved. As it is written: "The deliverer will come from Zion; he will turn godlessness away from Jacob. And this is my covenant with them when I take away their sins." (Romans 11:25-27 NIV)

That leads to the second question:

WHAT DOES THAT MEAN TO BELIEVERS?

We know that God brought Israel back into the land in 1948, and He will offer the New Covenant to them again when He returns to deal with their sins. We learn from their rejection that God had turned from the nation and appealed to individuals, including Gentiles. Jesus said that He was going to "build My church" on the basis of faith in His eternal atonement sacrifice and death, to ransom believers from the condemnation of the Law (see Matthew 16:18).

Salvation must begin with faith, not by works, as the Reformers learned and taught. What may not have been taught at that time was that our faith would lead to an indwelling of God's Holy Spirit (see Acts Chapter 2). But before that could happen, Jesus had to die and be resurrected in order to assume the High Priestly role of taking His own blood into the Holy of Holies in Heaven—thereby satisfying the justice of God (see 1 John 2:2). The Scriptures reveal that that took place for the first time on the Day of Pentecost. None of the New Covenant could have taken place until Jesus had died and was resurrected.

The Reformation did not dwell on when the church was formed. It was assumed to have been created in the covenant given to Abraham (see Genesis Chapter 15). The Catholic church from which they withdrew had been taught that they were an extension of Israel. That is why most of the major covenant churches believe the birth place or time was from Israel. As we have found in our reading of God's Word, three major passages of Scripture that support the Church, founded in Christianity, originated with: (1) Jesus stating that He was building His church on the foundation of faith (see Matthew 16:18), (2) His death, burial and resurrection to make an eternal atonement to remove us from condemnation for sin (see 1 John 2:2) and (3) to send the Holy Spirit to indwell believers, creating new minds and hearts (see Acts Chapter 2). The result was the creation of a Church known as a righteous family of God. That last feature was given to individuals, not corporately, to any church or nation.

Another application of grace for the new Church was the forming of a new creation, or Body of Christ, consisting of both Jews and Gentiles. The Church was to be seen metaphorically as a living building created from living stones, with Christ serving as the Cornerstone and capstone. Each individual was to be treated as a "living stone," vitally connected and directed by the Cornerstone. The entire building was to be indwelt or inhabited by the Father, Son and Holy Spirit living within them (see John 17:20-26).

A NEW APPLICATION FOR EACH BELIEVER

The cup and the covenant conveyed the love of God for all who believe. Its meaning to me is that He wants me to be a "living stone" in a new building He is building. I must be abiding in Christ first, and then be a living stone that is in communion with the Father, Son and Holy Spirit, toward an ultimate goal of eternal life in a new family God is creating. To be a proper "living stone," I must be in fellowship the other stones and completely in line with the cornerstone. I must be like Him in every way possible. There may be variations—in the order of service, the type of music that is preferred, the way the Eucharist is observed and forms used to baptize—without any living stone being discarded and while still being connected to the cornerstone.

The hope of this study was that we can find a unity of membership in the Church that Christ built and gave His life to make it a new creation, built on faith and the Word of God. Surely we share common ground as individuals, in whom a unity and love existing in us that exists in the Trinity. The choices we may make to differ on the music we appreciate, the manner in which we worship and identities we cherish as part of the reformation need not separate us.

To repeat, the New Covenant states that God wanted to regenerate us with new natures in righteous minds and hearts, given to us through faith in Christ along with an eternal forgiveness. In reality, it appears to mean that He is offering the kind of image to us as believers that we should have with one another. In honor to our common bond in Christ may we bring forth the promises of the New Covenant and teach them to our young. Thank you dear Lord for teachers like A. Wetherell Johnson and others who introduced us to the truth, that we believers are all "living stones" connected with and guided by the Spirit of the Cornerstone of God. Amen.

GUIDED DISCOVERY

Note: The emphasis of this last chapter is on the influence of the Cornerstone.

1. With Jesus as our "Cornerstone," what has been His greatest influence on you as a member of the Body of Christ?

2. How did the Apostle Paul explain in Romans 11:25-27 what God allowed to happen to Israel for not accepting Christ's offer of the New Covenant?

3. What did God do to extend His grace to Israelites willing to receive Christ?

4. Since the Cup (of Christ's suffering) was so vital to the fulfilling of the promises of the New Covenant, what is your response to His desire for you to be a living stone in the building of His church?

5. Write out your response to reading and studying *The Cup and The Covenant*, and share with others. Name a "living stone" that has been a supporter or influence on your growth in the Body of Christ.

Author's Response: I have two living stones that influenced me: A. Wetherell Johnson, to study the Bible, and Professor Ebeling, who taught me Doctrine and led my Ordination Council. I owe everything to the Father, Son and Holy Spirit for making me so aware of the riches of Grace.

Epilogue

An epilogue is a brief speech or story added at the end of a study or play, with information about something that preceded the research. This epilogue differs in that it describes something that occurred during the writing. The precedent was the story of a young man who felt the call to go back to school and study the history and the languages of the Bible. After he finished Bible school, he attended a university to attain a doctorate in Educational Psychology.

Most of his classes were organized around the topic of social interaction. A term kept emerging called *attitudes* and described in the early days as *feelings*. The more he read, the more fascinated he became because the term was inadequate to predict anything and something seemed to be lacking in its definition. The first thing he noticed was that without the word being directed toward or away from an object it was meaningless.

When it came time to select a topic to research and write about, the word *attitude* intrigued him. In his research from the literature he was reading and from what he had read in the Bible, he found that *faith* was an attitude. The main objects of faith were God, His Son Jesus or the Bible itself. From two years in Greek study, he had learned that the word *faith* was derived from two Greek words: one implying *believing in something* and the other *to feel about something*.

From his reading he had also learned there are two types of belief: *cognitive* and *affective*. An attitude must have both of them to be set apart like the word *faith*. Faith being an attitude can be held at one of three levels. The lowest is the *acceptance level*, with minimal motivation. The next level, and the first in which you can predict any drive toward an object, is called the *preference level*. Ultimately, the *commitment level* was where Paul and all the others lived, as seen in their lives. They were highly motivated toward Jesus. The student remembered a verse in Hebrews that used the word in that sense:

> And without faith it is impossible to please God, because anyone who comes to him must believe that he exists (cognitive) and that he rewards (affective belief) those who earnestly seek him (commitment). (Hebrews 11:6 NIV, Clarification mine)

He came to understand that faith comes from the mind and feelings from the heart of man. Combined, they describe the level to which a person is committed toward or away from the object (Christ). Paul must have made that same discovery when it dawned on Him what God had done with the New Covenant. He had rewarded those who had faith in Christ with righteous attitudes in their minds and hearts. The result was a new creation of believers that had the potential to emulate the attitudes of their savior, Jesus Christ.

> Love never fails. But where there are prophecies, they will cease; where there are tongues, they will be stilled; where there is knowledge, it will pass away. For we know in part and we prophesy in part, but when completeness comes, what is in part disappears. When I was a child, I talked like a child, I thought like a child, I reasoned like a child. When I became a man, I put the ways of childhood behind me. For now we see only a reflection as in a mirror; then we shall see face to face. Now I know in part; then I shall know fully, even as I am fully known. And now these three remain: faith, hope and love. But the greatest of these is love. (1 Corinthians 13:8-13 NIV)

The Cup and the Covenant, once understood, is the greatest love story ever told!

References

Bloom, B.S. Ed. (1956). *Taxonomy of educational objectives: Handbook I: Cognitive domain.* New York: David McKay.

Chafer, L.S. (1948). *Systematic theology: ecclesiology, Vol. IV.* Dallas, Texas: Dallas Seminary Press.

Krathwohl, D.R., Bloom, B.S., & Masia, B.B. (1964). *Taxonomy of educational objectives: Handbook II: Affective domain.* New York: David McKay.

Lewis, V. (1970). Prediction of academic performance from adolescent attitude-press organizations. *Journal of Educational Research, 63,* 204-208.

Lewis, V. & Narramore, B. (1990). *Cutting the cord: in adolescence.* Wheaton, Illinois: Tyndale House Publishers.

Lewis, V. (Spring 1974). A psychological analysis of faith. *Journal of Psychology and Theology, Vol. 2, No. 2.*

Acknowledgements

It is with deep gratitude that an acknowledgement be made of the great insights and scriptures suggested by Dr. Lewis Sperry Chafer in his Systematic Theology, Vol. V. publication. Equally important was the editing and comments made by Dr. Todd V. Lewis, PhD. Professor Emeritus of Biola University. Encouragement and insights came from my wife Vergene Lewis, retired Area Advisor, and Jackie Rettberg, former Teaching Leader for Miss A. Wetherell Johnson's Bible Study Fellowship classes.

A special thanks must be offered to Jonathan Price for his inspired cover design and the format of the book; the memory of a special visit to the Reformers Park in Worms, Germany with its statues of Martin Luther and John Knox, and the visit to the historical churches in Worms where Luther was tried. We are all indebted to our High Priest, The Lord Jesus Christ. Amen.

Made in the USA
Columbia, SC
09 December 2021

50820891R00126